HEADING NORTH

HEADING NORTH

LONDON MIDLAND STEAM
FROM EUSTON TO CARLISLE

ROD STEELE

The
History
Press

ACKNOWLEDGEMENTS

I would like to acknowledge the help and encouragement given to me by my family. Also my brother Ken for introducing his younger brother to loco spotting on a day which started my interest in railways.

To Glyn Shepherd for the Midland Region short works course comments, also Geoff Graham for recollections of events and the loan of material.

Special thanks go to David Loveday for allowing the extensive use of his photographs and Geoff Goslin for his valued assistance in sourcing material from the vast Gresley Society Collection.

My thanks are also due to these photographers: the late Gordon Coltas; Travel Lens Photographic; Geoff Goslin; Roger Carpenter; Ted Hancock; Lens of Sutton Collection and the 6201 Princess Elizabeth Society.

Any errors or omissions will be corrected in any future edition.

INTRODUCTION

For a generation of schoolboys the 1950s were wonderful times when events and personalities captured the imagination and gave many hours of entertainment. The Coronation in 1953 was enthusiastically welcomed, not only for the pageantry of the day but also for the removal of sweet rationing. The conquest of Everest, also in 1953, produced many aspiring Edmund Hillary moments for boys when conquering the nearest local hill.

Among the sporting heroes that inspired our young minds were footballers Stanley Matthews, Tom Finney, Bert Trautmann, Nat Lofthouse and Billy Wright. Many boys would re-enact goals or saves in the matches played on fields with coats being used as goalposts. In athletics Roger Bannister ran the mile in less than four minutes; the race home from school would beat the record in many a youngster's mind.

The toys of the '50s were bruised and battered Dinky racing cars with white balaclava-clad drivers; they would become Stirling Moss, Mike Hawthorn and Tony Brooks, all trying to beat Fangio to the finishing line. Sadly, many of the cars did not make the finishing line as they disappeared down a drain cover in the street.

Following a visit to the cinema to watch *Reach for the Sky* or *The Dam Busters*, there can be few boys who did not make an Airfix model of either a Hurricane or Spitfire. The larger kit of a Lancaster bomber was more expensive, so there were more schoolboy fighter pilots than bomber pilots at play.

Visits to the cinema were quite common as prices were affordable, and classics from Ealing Studios were shown such as *The Titfield Thunderbolt*, *The Ladykillers* and *The Lavender Hill Mob*, all entertaining huge audiences.

Eagerly awaited each week were the adventures of Luck of the Legion, PC 49 and Dan Dare who appeared in the pages of the *Eagle* comic. More humorous entertainment would be found in the *Beano* or the *Dandy*. Apart from all these diversions, probably the greatest hobby enjoyed by boys was the collecting of engine numbers, which were noted in logical form thanks to the *Ian Allan abc*, which for 2s 6d provided hours of entertainment. Armed with a pencil and *abc* spotter's book, the wonders of trainspotting took hold in what was to become one of the last decades of steam. Hours, days and weeks could be enjoyed by just observing trains at lineside or, sometimes, paying for a platform ticket to get closer to the engines at a station. At work on the railway were some pre-grouping veteran locos, still sporting their ex-LMS ownership while many engines had new liveries. Brunswick green was applied to express locos, lined black for mixed traffic types and plain black for freight classes. New classes began to appear as the BR Standard locos entered service on what was to be, in many cases, a ridiculously short working life. So by the late 1950s a full range of locomotive classes could be seen at work on the system before the advancement of the diesel era. For those who observed the steam days, the sight, smell and sound of a steam locomotive still lives on half a century later, especially when a preserved engine is seen in steam.

AN ESSENTIAL FOR ENTHUSIASTS ON ANY JOURNEY

First printed in 1942, the *abc* books were updated twice yearly until the last one in 1967; by then they had become a complete listing of all regions. At 2*s* 6*d* it would have been considered expensive, but for many youngsters the abc brought hours of pleasure. For many years the cover illustrations were excellent ink drawings of a loco of the relevant region, mostly drawn by A.N. Wolstenholme, but in later days these drawings gave way to a black and white photograph. As printing methods improved, colour plates of paintings began to appear as centre pages which in turn would be superseded by quality colour photograph centrefolds by the late 1950s.

One wonders if railway enthusiasm would have evolved to such a degree had Ian Allan not thought of the *abc* books.

The short works course in 1963 for the Midland Area as recalled by one attendee, consisted of visits to Crewe North Shed, Crewe Electric Depot, Rugby manual signal-box, Coventry automatic signal-box, the station announcer's room, Washwood Heath goods yard, Lawley Street goods depot and Sutton Park Signal School.

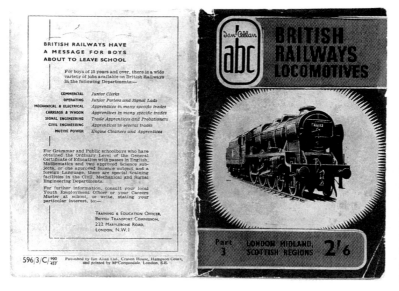

The 1957 summer edition of the Ian Allan Part 3 *abc* for the London Midland Region. A message for school leavers seeking apprenticeships is shown on the rear cover and makes interesting reading, although quite where a foreign language fitted into railway careers seems a bit mysterious.

WEST COAST MAIN LINE LOCOMOTIVES

The development of the steam locomotives we associate with the WCML originates in 1926. The London Midland & Scottish Railway somehow managed to borrow a Great Western Railway 'Castle' class engine for trials on the LMS. Working first on Euston to Crewe diagrams then to Carlisle, the results were so pleasing that a batch of fifty locomotives was ordered from the North British Locomotive Company straight off the drawing board. Plans of the Southern Railway's 'Lord Nelson' class were borrowed and a set of the GWR 'Castle' class were requested but refused.

The fifty engines built in 1927 were the Fowler 'Royal Scot' 4–6–0 class which, although rebuilt in later years, formed a mainstay of the LMS and later BR fleet of locomotives. So quickly were the class required that workshop capacity was stretched to the limits. Both the Queens Park Works and Hyde Park Works were used, with the first loco, no. 6100, emerging from Queens Park in July 1927. By November 1927 the order for fifty had been completed.

The engines proved a great success with 'The Royal Scot' train on the non-stop run between Euston and Carlisle of 299 miles hauling fifteen coaches. So pleased with the results were the LMS, that they increased the class by twenty more engines, ordered from their Derby Works in 1929, with a completion date of 1930.

Some years later, problems with smokebox leakage and frames hastened rebuilding as the taper boiler version. The first to be treated was no. 6103 in 1943; the last of the class was no. 46137 in 1955.

The 'Claughton' class 4–6–0 engines were deemed both uneconomical on coal consumption and maintenance costs. The three-cylinder layout of the 'Royal Scot' class had made a favourable impression; so much so that a smaller version was evolved as accountancy rebuilds. Of the original design, the Fowler-style cabs were retained on all engines, some driving wheels were reused and even then on just a few engines. The loco class was to be known as 'Patriot', but common naming yielded the Baby Scot nickname.

The appointment of a GWR man in 1932, (Sir) William Stanier, resulted in the locomotive fleet that the LMS had always wished for. His designs were to transform the LMS and some lasted to the very end of steam services in 1968. From the outset, all Stanier engines were to have taper boilers and Belpaire fireboxes.

The first design of the regime was the Crewe-built 4–6–2, with a total of twelve introduced in 1933 and known as the 7P 'Princess' class. The class number was never enlarged as experience gained was used in the later Stanier 'Pacifics'. One experimental loco based on the 'Princess' was no. 6202 built in 1935, the unique Turbomotive.

Other classes followed in rapid succession with forty of the Stanier 5F version of 2–6–0 in 1933 from Crewe Works. Also, after problems with superheating were resolved, the 191 'Jubilee' class engines introduced in 1934 proved capable performers in the 5XP class. The

Stanier's Express Locomotives

'Jubilee' no. 45658 alongside rebuilt 'Royal Scot' no. 46127. *(Travel Lens Photographic)*

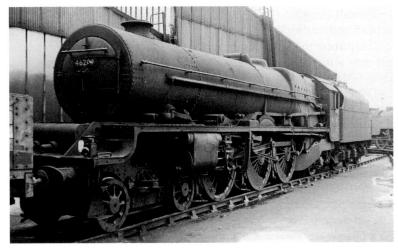

'Princess' class no. 46209 *Princess Beatrice.* *(R.S. Collection)*

'Duchess' no. 46234 *Duchess of Abercorn.* *(R.S. Collection)*

5XP 4–6–0, introduced from 1934 and continuing in production with modifications until 1951, eventually totalled 842. It was instantly popular with loco men. That the loco was capable of pulling any train on the LMS was an opinion voiced by many railwaymen of the wonderful ubiquitous 'Black 5s'.

Appearing in 1934, a class of thirty-seven Derby-built 3-cylinder 4P 2–6–4 tank engines again proved successful. The Stanier version supplemented the well-liked Fowler design which was very powerful and had a good turn of speed.

In 1945 a further 277 engines were ordered to the design of Charles Fairburn, who for a short time succeeded Stanier as Chief Mechanical Engineer (CME). The appearance was similar but with a reduced wheelbase and lack of upright plating in front of the cylinders.

Attention for the need of a class 8F 2–8–0 heavy freight engine resulted in 852 examples between 1935 and 1943. Some of the class saw military service with the War Department and nos 48246–48263 were returned into BR stock some years after. Several engines were lost in service, one of which still lies in a shipwreck off the Egyptian coast and now attracts the attention of scuba-divers.

Another 1935 introduction were 206 members of the 2-cylinder class 4P 2–6–4 tank engine, mostly built at Derby until 1943, while the least successful of all Stanier's engines were the 1935-built class 3P 2–6–2 tank engines. Along with his predecessor's 2–6–4T, they were both considered underboilered.

The publicity value of a streamlined engine to compete with the LNER's A4 4–6–2s was a priority with the directors of the LMS. Although never favoured by Stanier, the streamlined 7P 4–6–2 class was introduced in 1937 with nos 46220–6224 finished in blue and silver livery. In 1938, nos 6225–46229 were finished in maroon and gilt, followed later that year by non-streamlined nos 6230–46234. Two further batches of streamliners arrived in 1939 and 1940, firstly nos 6235–6239 and 6240–6244, again in the maroon livery. Wartime builds in 1943 were streamlined nos 6245–6248, but in wartime black livery.

The 1944 builds of nos 6249–6252 were non-streamlined and finished in black. Then the post-war LMS livery of black with maroon and straw lining was applied to the 1946 batch of the non-streamlined nos 6253–6255.

Fittingly the last LMS 'Pacific' 4–6–2, by now modified by H. Ivatt, was no. 46256 and was named in honour of the Chief Mechanical Engineer whose designs transformed the company, *Sir William A. Stanier F.R.S.*

The final member of the class built in BR days was no. 46257 another, Ivatt modification of 1948. To enthusiasts the nickname of 'Duchess' referred to the class, even though only ten were actually named after a duchess.

Also attributed to Stanier were the rebuilt 'Royal Scot', rebuilt 'Patriot' and two rebuilt 'Jubilee' class engines.

The last Chief Mechanical Engineer of the LMS, Ivatt, was responsible for some very creditable designs of 2–6–2 tank engines and 2–6–0 tender engines; some were slightly modified to eventually become BR Standard types.

With nationalisation in 1948, future locomotive building was to use standard parts for economical reasons. Of the express design 4–6–2s the 'Britannia' and 'Clan' classes, together with the solitary no. 71000 *Duke of Gloucester* saw use on the WCML but never achieved the popularity with enthusiasts that the Stanier engines had.

Altogether, the short-lived Standards were to number 999 locomotives.

A LOOK AROUND LONDON EUSTON

Before making their way over to the departure side of the station, most enthusiasts make time to call at the arrival platforms to view any incoming expresses. Platforms one and two prove the most popular as it is on these lines that the best views can be obtained. Between platforms two and three, a long line of the familiar London black cabs await arriving passengers.

For the spotters, a feast of the best of London Midland motive power presents itself with the mighty 'Duchess', 'Princess', 'Royal Scot', 'Patriot' and 'Jubilee' class engines. Bringing in empty carriages and removing coaching stock are locos from 1A Willesden Shed.

In the early evening the area around platform two becomes a hive of activity, all concerned with loading the renowned Down Night Mail, probably the most important train on the whole system. This will invariably be hauled by a 'Duchess' or to give it its proper title, a 'Princess Coronation Pacific' loco.

As National Service was still in place in the 1950s, a common sight is uniformed members of the armed forces making journeys back to base, or homeward bound on leave. Burly military police with distinctive red caps make their presence known to servicemen and keep a check on travel warrants and leave times; offenders will be reported and face charges on return to bases.

Walking towards the far side of the station, platforms four and five reveal the direct current rails for units on the Watford electrified service. Platform six is worth a look as this houses the stationmaster's office and sees use for the occasional Royal Train specials, codenamed the 'Grove'.

The middle platforms of Euston can prove a disappointment, as it always appears to be a jumble of platforms more concerned with parcels traffic than passengers.

Entry to the departure side is through a barrier where tickets are inspected before being allowed onto platforms twelve to fifteen. Not as imposing or photographically pleasing as the arrivals side of the station, the platforms are very narrow and soon become cluttered with passengers, luggage and catering supplies for the trains.

At the buffers end of the platforms, by the Menzies Bookstall, the 1A loco that has brought in the empty stock will remain coupled to the train to provide steam heat for the carriages. When the train engine backs down from 1B Camden Shed and couples onto its stock, the pilot engine will then uncouple, leaving the express engine to provide the heating.

Impressive are the variety of named trains to depart from these platforms. Named trains warranted, in most cases, a named engine much to the delight of spotters.

Titled Train Departures from Euston

Scotland
'The Royal Scot' to Glasgow Central
'The Mid-Day Scot' to Glasgow Central
'The Caledonian' to Glasgow Central
'The Royal Highlander' (sleeper car train) to Perth, Aberdeen/Inverness

Wales
'The Welshman' to Llandudno/Pwllheli

Ireland
'The Irish Mail' (via Holyhead)
'The Shamrock' (via Liverpool Lime Street)
'The Emerald Isle Express' (via Holyhead)
'The Ulster Express' (via Fleetwood, later Heysham)
'The Northern Irishman' (sleeping car train) via Stranraer

Wolverhampton (High Level)
'The Midlander'

Liverpool
'The Merseyside Express' to Liverpool Lime Street
'The Red Rose' to Liverpool Lime Street
(also boat train specials)
'Empress Voyager' (when required)
'Cunard Express' (when required)
'The Manxman' (summers only)

Manchester
'The Mancunian' to Manchester London Road
'The Comet' (via Stoke on Trent) to Manchester London Road
'The Lancastrian' to Manchester London Road

The Lake District
'The Lakes Express' to Windermere

Headboards of Anglo-Scottish trains

Pride of place in the named trains list are the most important Anglo-Scottish 10 a.m. and 1 p.m. departures, 'The Royal Scot' and 'The Mid-Day Scot'. Although some express trains were titled and carried coach destination boards before British Railways became nationalised, they did not carry headboards until BR days.

The most ornate design, probably dating from the early 1950s, featured a red lion rampant on a shield and yellow lettering of 'Royal Scot' with a tartan background. 'The Royal Scot' was inaugurated in 1927.

The standard curved design, used on many BR headboards, was introduced between 1951 and 1953. Background colours varied from black, red and the Scottish region's version of light blue.

'The Caledonian' was a newly titled limited-load express introduced in June 1957 and remained as a service until September 1964. Several versions of the headboard exist although all have the common white lettering on a red background. The two shields feature the cross of St Andrew and that of St George.

Introduced in 1951, only one style of headboard was ever carried by 'The Mid-Day Scot'. The only variation was in the background colours, which were either red or light blue. The title originated in 1927 and was commonly known to railwaymen as the Corridor due to the train being the first to use corridor coaches.

THE
MID-DAY SCOT

WEEKDAYS

NORTHBOUND				SOUTHBOUND		
dep	1	0	pm	LONDON (EUSTON)	arr	10	12	pm
				WATFORD JUNCTION	arr	9	43	pm
dep	2	37	pm	RUGBY			
dep	4	14	pm	CREWE	dep	7	7	pm
				PRESTON	dep	5	47	pm
				LANCASTER	dep	5	18	pm
dep	7	27	pm	CARLISLE	dep	3	50	pm
arr	8	56	pm	CARSTAIRS	dep	2	24	pm
arr	9	23	pm	MOTHERWELL	dep	1	36	pm
arr	9	45	pm	GLASGOW (CENTRAL)	dep	1	15	pm

BRITISH RAILWAYS

THE
ROYAL SCOT

WEEKDAYS

NORTHBOUND

LONDON (EUSTON)	dep	10	0	am
GLASGOW (CENTRAL)	arr	6	25	pm

SOUTHBOUND

GLASGOW (CENTRAL)	dep	10	0	am
LONDON (EUSTON)	arr	6	13	pm

BRITISH RAILWAYS

A Typical Mid-1950s Euston Morning of Principal Trains

Departures

00.02	Crewe	5A	RS
00.20	Glasgow	1B	D
00.30	Liverpool	8A	PR
00.40	Manchester	8A	J
01.37	Wolverhampton	9A	J
07.55	Liverpool	1B	D
08.30	Manchester	9A	RS
08.50	Wolverhampton	1B	J
09.00	Wolverhampton	3B	J
09.45	Manchester	9A	RS
10.00	Glasgow	1B	D
10.40	Carlisle	1B	D
10.50	Blackpool	1B	RS
11.45	Manchester	9A	RS

Arrivals

01.10	Crewe	5A	RS
01.37	Birmingham	1B	J
02.40	Liverpool	8A	PR
03.04	Manchester	9A	RS
03.32	Windermere	1B	RS
04.00	Glasgow	5A	RS
04.30	Kendal	5A	RS
05.05	Glasgow	1B	RS
05.24	Manchester	9A	RS
05.57	Liverpool	8A	RS
06.30	Holyhead	7C	RS
06.50	Glasgow	12A	D
07.03	Glasgow	1B	D
07.13	Perth	1B	RS
07.20	Glasgow	1B	D
08.05	Stranraer	1B	RS
08.20	Inverness	5A	D
09.56	Wolverhampton	3B	J
10.30	Wolverhampton	3B	J
11.09	Crewe	5A	D
11.25	Manchester	9A	RS
11.35	Heysham	1B	RS

KEY TO SHEDS
1B Camden, 3B Bushbury, 5A Crewe, 7C Holyhead (6J 1952–66), 8A Edge Hill, 9A Longsight, 12A Carlisle Upperby (12B 1948–50 then 12A 1950–8 and then 12B again 1958–66) and 24E Blackpool.

Euston Afternoon Principal Services

Departures

12.30	Liverpool	8A	PR
12.50	Wolverhampton	3B	J
13.30	Glasgow	5A	D
13.35	Blackpool	24E	J
14.20	Wolverhampton	3B	J
14.30	Liverpool	8A	RS
14.45	Manchester	9A	RS
15.00	Birmingham	1B	J
15.45	Manchester	9A	J
16.30	Manchester	1B	RS
16.37	Wolverhampton	3B	J
16.55	Liverpool	8A	RS
17.05	Blackpool	1B	RS
17.35	Holyhead	5A	RS
17.50	Wolverhampton	3B	J

Arrivals

12.00	Liverpool	8A	PR
12.41	Wolverhampton	3B	J
12.48	Manchester	9A	RS
12.55	Blackpool	1B	RS
13.05	Manchester	9A	RS
13.20	Holyhead	7C	RS
13.30	Wolverhampton	3B	J
13.45	Liverpool	8A	PR
13.55	Manchester	9A	RS
14.30	Wolverhampton	3B	J
14.45	Liverpool	8A	J
15.05	Blackpool	1B	J
15.37	Llandudno	5A	J
15.45	Manchester	9A	J
16.12	Carlisle	1B	D
16.34	Wolverhampton	1B	J
17.15	Glasgow	1B	D
17.45	Liverpool	8A	RS
17.54	Manchester	9A	RS

KEY TO LOCO CLASSES
D – Duchess, PR – Princess Royal, J – Jubilee, RS – Royal Scot. As the BR standard classes emerged they were introduced on some services. The 'Britannia' class engines are the most noticeable of all BR types.

Euston Evening Principal Services

Arrivals					Departures			
					18.00	Manchester	9A	RS
					18.10	Liverpool	8A	PR
					18.20	Heysham	1B	RS
18.30	Wolverhampton	1B	J		18.30	Preston	5A	D
					18.55	Wolverhampton	3B	J
					19.00	Birmingham	5A	RS
					19.20	Inverness	1B	RS
19.26	Perth	1B	D					
					19.30	Perth	1B	D
19.52	Manchester	9A	RS					
20.20	Liverpool	8A	RS					
					20.30	Glasgow (TPO)	5A	D
20.50	Liverpool	1B	D		20.50	Holyhead	7C	RS
21.00	Glasgow	1B	D					
					21.10	Glasgow	1B	D
21.20	Manchester	9A	RS					
					21.25	Glasgow	12A	D
					21.35	Birmingham	1B	J
					22.00	Manchester	9A	RS
					22.45	Manchester	9A	RS
					22.52	Perth	7C	RS
23.04	Blackpool	24E	J					
					23.05	Windermere	5A	J
					23.50	Glasgow	1B	RS

(TPO) is the Travelling Post Office, also known as the West Coast Postal or the 'Night Mail'.

Some expresses warrant relief trains when required as is the case with 'The Royal Scot', which in the late 1950s had a relief train departing at 09.50, ten minutes before the main train.

As can be noted from the timetables, Euston was not bustling with traffic for much of the time, but was always impressive in the named engines that arrived and departed. Probably the largest number of sightings is the 'Royal Scot' and rebuilt 'Patriot' classes. By the early 1960s it was commonplace to see trains diesel-hauled on expresses that once were steam duties.

THE NIGHT MAIL

The only train to leave from the arrival platforms at Euston was, for the major part of its journey, not for passengers: it was the 'Night Mail' or to give it its proper title, the 'North Western Night Up Travelling Post Office'. Probably the most important train on the WCML, it commenced the journey at 8.30 p.m. each evening and demanded strict timekeeping en route.

The train was normally hauled by a Crewe North 'Duchess' for the first leg of the journey between Euston and Glasgow Central. As the train was timed to connect with other mail trains on the system, lateness was not acceptable.

Preparation for the train began with the stock from the previous night being taken to the triangle to turn at Willesden, a requirement owing to the special pick up, receiving apparatus and lighting situated on the coaches' left-hand side. The train would then be brought in to platform two at around 7.00 p.m. by a Willesden loco. The stock consisted of around fourteen mail vans, five of which were specifically dedicated for sorting, picking up and delivering leather-bound satchels at speed, while the other nine were used as stowage vans.

For one and a half hours, post office vans from all over London utilised the taxi road of platform two. This allowed both sorted and unsorted sacks to be rapidly loaded onboard. Provision for late post was made with a letterbox on the side of a coach; for this service a □d late surcharge was charged.

The GPO staffed the train with forty to fifty workers each evening. Once on board they would set about sorting the post into the numerous sections of labelled pigeonholes. Each worker was allocated forty-eight of these sections.

Sorted into destination areas, the mail was packed securely into the leather pouches for delivery at speed to special attachments along the line. The attachments, situated at thirty-three locations along the WCML, were manned by post office workers who hung pouches of mail for pick up on the lineside apparatus in readiness for the train, and swing it outwards as it approached. At various times during the night, postmen would make their way along narrow paths to load mail pouches onto the thirty-three automatic exchange locations. A small hut was provided for the postman to await the train's arrival and a set of steps to load the lineside catchers. A careful check on the time was required in order to extend the arms at the correct timing to connect with the mail train.

Standing well clear of the track, the postman would see the train, illuminated by a string of lights, approaching at speed. As the train approached, a chequered board indicated the location of a lineside pick-up point. Mechanical arms were extended, the first to pick up incoming mail, which detached into a net extended from the train. A second arm, this with outgoing mail, was also extended to connect with another lineside catcher, which detached the pouch into a trackside net.

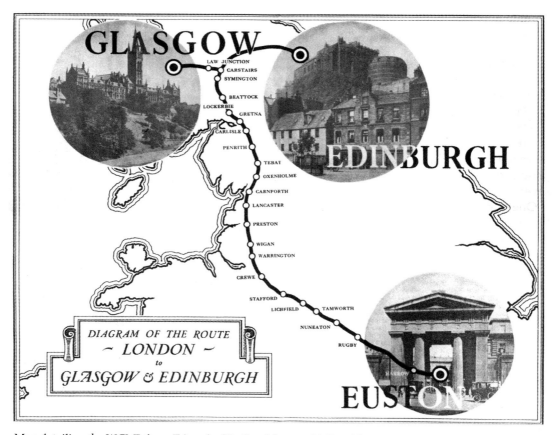

Map detailing the WCML from *Triumph of the Royal Scot*, an LMS publication of 1933.

Several thuds would be heard as the equipment connected and sacks of mail would be propelled into the waiting lineside net, while the other catcher delivered incoming mail into the nets on board the train.

The first stop for the train was at Rugby, 82 miles from Euston, where a four-minute stop allowed a connection with the Peterborough Mail train. The next stop of nine minutes was at Tamworth Low Level in the Trent Valley. Trains from Bristol to Birmingham and Lincoln, Nottingham to Derby ran into Tamworth High Level where an exchange took place.

At Crewe, a stop of sixteen minutes allowed the engine to be changed. Meanwhile, the permanent postal workers based here hurried to load and interchange mail from other postal specials from Swansea, Manchester, Stoke, Shrewsbury and Holyhead.

At Preston another stop was made, this for ten minutes to accommodate mail from and to Lancashire. From Preston, the 'Postal' continued to Carlisle for a 3.12 a.m. arrival. After a ten-minute stop when coaches were attached and detached for Scottish destinations, the train arrived in Glasgow at 5.27 a.m.

The superb next-day postal delivery came to an end when transportation of mail by rail was transferred to road vehicles. The last lineside exchange of mail took place in October 1971 and the last TPO ran in January 2004.

The Great Train Robbery

An event on 8 August 1963 that became front-page national news for months was the Great Train Robbery at Sears Crossing on the WCML. The thieves in the gang engineered a dummy signal to bring the train to a stop and offload an enormous amount of banknotes, estimated at £2.6 million, which were on board. The hoard, even by today's values is a large sum, but in 1963 this was an absolute fortune.

After an intensive police search, the gang's hideout was discovered and evidence found there led to some arrests. Others fled the country but eventually all those involved served prison sentences, which in comparison with other crimes appeared to many as draconian in severity.

One of the robbers, Ronnie Biggs, after escaping from prison, fled to Brazil and although the police tracked him down they were unable to extradite him due to Brazilian laws. Afterwards it transpired that the gang had recruited someone who was supposed to have locomotive driving experience. The TPO train was at this time diesel-hauled; the gang's driver proved of no use as he had only ever driven steam locos.

1

THE WEST COAST MAIN LINE

Our journey will take us the 299 miles to Carlisle, although the full length of the route is 401 miles to end in Scotland at Glasgow Central station. Commencing at London Euston station, we board a northbound train from the far-from-welcoming departure platforms. Generally, express trains travelling this distance have the benefit of one of Sir William Stanier's powerful 'Pacific' locomotives and possibly a change of engine will take place on reaching Crewe 158 miles along the line.

The cramped engine shed of Camden 1B is visited to view the locos on show. As Camden's rosters are for express passenger trains, the engines on shed are express types capable of hauling fast, heavy trains. Then at Willesden we call into the 1A depot and see the huge variety of both passenger and goods engines which are serviced there.

Approaching Bushey, a wavy line notice and an S notice show the engine's fireman where to lower the tender's scoop into the water troughs, and we pick up around 2,000 gallons in just a few hundred yards without slowing. As express engines use around 40 gallons of water for each mile travelled, the tender's water capacity has to be refilled regularly and there are nine sets of troughs on the way to Carlisle.

After 82 miles, Rugby Midland is passed. The station is vast and has a span of fourteen lines; one of its platforms is so long it can accommodate twenty-four-coach trains. Across the line, the huge GEC electrical engineering company advertises its presence. Rugby Loco Shed is passed, its allocation includes less powerful engines and the largest shedded there are the 'Black 5s'. It is always worth a look out for any engines destined to enter the Rugby Locomotive Testing Plant; these could come from any part of the system. The loco on test runs on rollers with the fireman feeding measured amounts of coal into the firebox.

'The Midlander' two-hour express for Wolverhampton leaves the WCML at Rugby. The Trent Valley Railway also starts at Rugby and runs through to Stafford, a distance of 51 miles.

The stations along the line are designated as first and second class. Designed by the architect John Livock, so-called first-class stations are those at Atherstone–Lichfield and Tamworth and are built in what could be described as a Tudor/Jacobean style with superbly ornate chimneys. Second-class stations are timber-clad; Brinklow and Shilton have brick outers on road-facing walls. Nuneaton started life as a second-class station but was later upgraded to become first.

A peculiar arrangement at Atherstone is the signal-box, which is built on a narrow brick pillar and accessed by a girder bridge that straddles the lines. The signals along the Trent Valley vary in design, but have a number which are very tall so as not to be obscured by bridges. At Tamworth the line is crossed by the Derby to Birmingham line and clusters of trainspotters are attracted to the field beside the Tamworth Low Level station.

On reaching Colwich some trains leave the WCML and travel to Stoke-on-Trent and Manchester.

The end of the Trent Valley is Stafford which is approached by a sharp curve. The Castle Engine Works of W.G. Bagnall, builders of many export locomotives as well as LMS 'Jinty' tanks, lie alongside the line.

The 25 miles between Stafford and Crewe includes the section where the LMS captured the World Speed Record. The speed of 114mph achieved by (4)6220 *Coronation* in 1937 was soon to be beaten by the LNER's *Mallard* with 126mph. That a 'Duchess' was indeed capable of more cannot be disputed; the problem lay in the LMS not having a long enough straight stretch of line where the engine could be opened to full regulator.

Crewe has several junctions; at Crewe South lines to Shrewsbury go west, and there's an east junction to Stoke-on-Trent. At the north end of Crewe the east junction is for North Wales and the west junction for Manchester.

The line now follows the flat Cheshire plains; Liverpool-bound trains leave the WCML at Weaver Junction. Our train now has a sharp rise and fall to negotiate in order to pass over the Manchester Ship Canal and then on to Wigan and Preston. Preston is the branch for ex-Lancashire and Yorkshire Railway lines and immediately after leaving the station we pass Preston Loco Shed in the shadows of a very imposing church steeple. The route taken by thousands of holidaymakers to Blackpool is to the west of the church.

After 21 miles, a sharp descent of 1 in 188 leads into Lancaster Castle station. The castle is to the right of the train while the other landmark is the huge grey gasholder (unlike many that rise and fall, this type always stays at the same height).

From Lancaster the footplate crews have their hardest work to do with long climbs to overcome. About 3 miles from Lancaster we have the one and only glimpse of the coast, even though the line is named the West Coast Main Line. This is at Hest Bank where Morecambe Bay can be seen for just a few moments.

At Carnforth there are junctions for Barrow in the west and Leeds in the east. The climbs commence at Carnforth with 2□ miles at 1 in 134, followed by a fairly easy section until Milnthorpe is passed. From Milnthorpe a climb of 13 miles graded between 1 in 106 and 1 in 175 brings us to Grayrigg.

For a short time the line is almost level, giving the footplate crew the opportunity to get the fire in order for the climb of one of the steepest lines in the country, Shap, which is at 916ft above sea level. The last chance to scoop the water troughs at Dillicar is made and the driver now has to decide if a stop is needed to summon one of Tebay's 2-6-4 tank engines for a push up to Shap Summit. Tebay has a small number of tank engines available as bankers for northbound trains if requested. Not all engines will need a banker; if the load and fire condition is in order, some drivers make the climb unassisted to save time. The residents of the railway cottages at Tebay are accustomed to the cacophony of engine whistles both day and night.

The climb up Shap begins and gradients vary from 1 in 145 to a cruel 1 in 75 for the last 4 miles before the summit is reached. The footplate crew will be pleased to crest the summit as this heralds an easy 32-mile run, nearly all downhill, until Carlisle comes into view with ancient and modern structures of the cathedral, the castle, factory chimneys and the city's gas holders. For us it is journey's end, for the train a change of engine and for the footplate crew a rest period before making the same journey, but this time southbound.

The Route from London Euston to Crewe

London Euston ⇒

Willesden 5 miles ⇒ Wembley 8 miles ⇒

Harrow & Wealdstone 11 miles ⇒ Hatch End 13 miles ⇒

Bushey Troughs ⇒ Bushey & Oxhey 16 miles ⇒ Watford 17 miles ⇒

Kings Langley 21 miles ⇒ Apsley 23 miles ⇒ Hemel Hempstead 24 miles ⇒

Berkhampsted 28 miles ⇒ Tring 31 miles ⇒ Cheddington 36 miles ⇒

Leighton Buzzard 40 miles ⇒ Bletchley 46 miles ⇒Wolverton 52 miles ⇒

Castlethorpe Troughs ⇒ Castlethorpe 55 miles ⇒ Roade 60 miles ⇒

Blisworth 62 miles ⇒ Weedon 70 miles ⇒ Welton 75 miles ⇒

Rugby Midland 82 miles ⇒ *Newbold Troughs* ⇒ Brinklow 88 miles ⇒

Shilton 91 miles ⇒ Nuneaton 97 miles ⇒ Atherstone 102 miles ⇒

Polesworth 106 miles ⇒ Tamworth LL ⇒ *Hademore Troughs* ⇒

Lichfield TV 116 miles ⇒ Armitage 121 miles ⇒ Rugeley 124 miles ⇒

Colwich 127 miles ⇒ Stafford 133 miles ⇒ Norton Bridge 138 miles ⇒

Whitmore Troughs ⇒ Crewe 158 miles

(Water pick-up points are indicated in *italics*)
With the exception of the Manchester-bound 'Comet' and the Wolverhampton-bound 'Midlander', all premier express train departures from London Euston travelled through Crewe.

The Route from Crewe to Carlisle

Crewe 158 miles (from Euston) ⇒

Winsford 165 miles ⇒ Hartford 170 miles ⇒ Acton Bridge 172 miles ⇒

Weaver Junction ⇒ *Moore Troughs* ⇒ Warrington Bank Quay 182 miles ⇒

Golborne 190 miles ⇒ Wigan 194 miles ⇒ Coppull 199 miles ⇒

Balshaw Lane & Euxton 202 miles ⇒ Leyland 205 Miles ⇒

Farrington 206 miles ⇒ Preston 209 miles ⇒ *Brock Troughs* ⇒

Garstang & Catterall 218 miles ⇒ Lancaster 230 miles ⇒

Hest Bank 233 miles ⇒ *Hest Bank Troughs* ⇒ Bolton le Sands 234 miles ⇒

Carnforth 236 miles ⇒ Milnthorpe 243 miles ⇒ Oxenhope 249 miles ⇒

Grayrigg 256 miles ⇒ Low Gill 258 miles ⇒ *Dillicar Troughs* ⇒

Tebay 262 miles ⇒ Shap Summit 267 miles ⇒ Shap 269 miles ⇒

Penrith 281 miles ⇒ *Carlisle Citadel 299 miles*

(Water pick-up points are indicated in *italics*)

(Glasgow 401 miles)

2

EUSTON ARRIVALS

Above: 'Princess Royal' class 4–6–2 no. 46203 *Princess Margaret Rose* heads into Euston's platform one with 'The Shamrock', one of the heavy London expresses from Liverpool, on 8 May 1960. *(R.S. Collection)*

Right: 'Jubilee' 4–6–0 no. 45578 *United Provinces* has a solitary spectator as she enters into platform two with what is probably one of the Manchester expresses. *(R.S. Collection)*

Jubilee no. 45741 *Leinster* enters Euston with 'The Midlander', the two-hour Birmingham to Euston service. Meanwhile, on platform two a Fowler 2–6–4 tank engine is coupling up to the coaching stock of an earlier arrival to remove it for servicing. *(R.S. Collection)*

Opposite, bottom: Nuneaton 2B-based Hughes/Fowler Crab 2–6–0 no. 42891 is light-engine at Euston on 28 December 1959, probably to couple onto empty stock for removal to the carriage sidings at Willesden. Crabs were layered in grime for most of their days, but when new some carried the crimson lake passenger livery. *(R.S. Collection)*

'Jinty' 0–6–0T no. 47514 of 1B Camden Shed is seen on pilot duties at Euston. Although express locos made up the majority of Camden's locos, around twelve 'Jinty' tanks were always included in 1B allocations. *(R.S. Collection)*

Manchester Longsight's 9A 'Royal Scot' no. 46111 *Royal Fusilier* awaits the 'right away' to push her train out of Euston before going on-shed at Camden. *(R.S. Collection)*

Opposite, top: Unnamed 'Patriot' no. 45513 gives a push to a departing express. The engine will drop away from the train at the top of Camden Bank, 1 mile distant. On the platform behind, passengers are about to board a departure headed by no. 46245 *City of London. (R.S. Collection)*

Opposite, bottom: Very American in both design and colour, the prototype 3000hp Deltic brings 'The Merseyside Express' into platform one. With the planned electrification of Liverpool services, the production run of BR Deltics became popular motive power on the Eastern Region. *(Gresley Society)*

There is a wealth of detail – such as barrows, a Scammel Inter-station parcel truck and an old car – around no. 46207 *Princess Arthur of Connaught*, arriving with the 'The Merseyside Express' on 18 July 1958. *(R.S Collection)*

Opposite, top: A double-headed arrival into platform four in April 1963 sees Stanier 'Black 5' 4–6–0 no. 45299 of 1E Bletchley Shed ahead of a Stanier 4–6–0 unidentified 'Jubilee'. A diesel in the background indicates steam's decline setting in. *(D. Loveday)*

Opposite, bottom: Although classed as a 'Royal Scot', no. 46170 *British Legion* was a rebuild of the ill-fated 6399 Fowler High Pressure locomotive *Fury*, withdrawn in 1930. In appearance, no. 46170 looks like a 'Royal Scot' but has a non-standard boiler to the rest of her classmates and a Stanier design of cab. The nameplate of the engine was large and had a unique design of the badge of the British Legion. Pictured at 4.10 p.m. one day in 1959, Euston appears to be deserted except for the black Morris or Standard car parked by the wall of platform one. *(R.S. Collection)*

'The Merseyside Express' from Liverpool Lime Street, hauled by leader of the class no. 46200 *The Princess Royal* of 8A Edge Hill, rests at buffer stops on platform one. *(R.S. Collection)*

'Duchess' 4–6–2 no. 46237 *City of Bristol* takes centre stage for the classic Euston arrivals photograph in August 1962. The curved sweep of the roof and platform edge are always a favourite of photographers. On the right in the background and on the left are the ever-present parcels vans and the London black cabs of the era. *(D. Loveday)*

The driver of rebuilt 'Patriot' no. 45540 *Sir Robert Turnbull* waits for parcels to be unloaded before backing down to Camden Shed and pushing the empty stock up the bank in 1960. The safety valves lifting are against regulations in a station, but could be due to the driver having to make up lost time and having a healthy fire at the end of the trip. *(R.S. Collection)*

Rebuilt 'Patriot' no. 45530 *Sir Frank Ree* amid the steelwork during the rebuilding of Euston station. The buffer stops of platform one have been re-sited during construction work. The 'Patriot' wears a 1A Willesden shedplate, which dates the photograph to between 1962 and 1964. She was reallocated to Holyhead in 1964, then Carlisle Kingmoor until withdrawal in 1966 as the last member of the class. *(R.S. Collection)*

An early 1950s departure of 'The Mid-Day Scot' headed by no. 46206 *Princess Marie Louise*. The loco was later to have separate top-feed and domes fitted and was the only 'Princess' to have a tender coal pusher. *(R.S. Carpenter)*

Opposite, top: Deep into the narrow parcels platforms of Euston, a grimy no. 46256 *Sir William Stanier F.R.S.* is seen alongside some crates labelled for Wolverton. The crates could possibly contain the specially polished buffers and draw hook kept at Wolverton for fitting to 'Pacific' locos on royal duties from Camden. *(R.S. Collection)*

Opposite, bottom: Edge Hill's no. 46206 *Princess Marie Louise* awaits her return to Liverpool; unusually the loco carries no headboard. On the adjacent platform 'Duchess' no. 46238 *City of Carlisle* is also coupled up in readiness for a northbound departure. *(R.S. Collection)*

Unnamed 'Patriot' no. 45510 makes her way out of the station on 3 October 1959; a 24L shedplate shows the loco's new allocation to Carnforth. On the right-hand side we are able to see some quite rare details of the far side of Euston. *(R.S. Collection)*

The sanders are in use on no. 46201 *Princess Elizabeth* as she pulls away. A grubby rebuilt 'Patriot' no. 45526 *Morecambe and Heysham* on the right is also ready to get under way. The 5A shed code and early BR logo dates the photograph to about 1954. *(R.S. Collection)*

3

DEPARTURE FROM EUSTON

As departure time approaches an increased level of activity can be observed. Before boarding, adults visit the bookstall to purchase a magazine or newspaper, whereas younger travellers will search for railway literature such as the *abc* spotters books or *I Spy on a Railway Journey* booklets.

The guard makes his way to the front of the train to inform the driver of the load and also to confirm departure and arrivals for stations en route. Some passengers dash to board the train after arriving at Euston at the last minute.

Before departure it is noticeable that many passengers, after locating their seats in the coaching stock, then leave the coach and wander to the front of the train to see what locomotive is to head the train. For a short experimental period time a small label displaying the driver's name on the cab side of the loco was the practice.

Family and friends cluster next to the coaches in order to say their goodbyes; many hold handkerchiefs for waving or wiping away a tear. The noise of coach doors being closed precedes the shrill of a whistle indicating that all doors are secured and the train is ready for departure. The train's driver gives an answering whistle from the engine.

A cloud of steam normally envelopes the front of the locomotive as the cylinder drain valves are opened. Noisy and spectacular, this operation is to empty any water build-up in the cylinders caused by steam turning to water when the locomotive is stationary. It also startles many onlookers.

As the driver gently opens the regulator, a little wheel slip generally happens as the loco's driving wheels gain adhesion. Slowly the train gets under way with banking assistance from the 1A engine that has brought in the empty carriages and heated the train prior to the express engine coupling up. The start of a journey from Euston is difficult, as in the first mile of the journey gradients of 1 in 70 and 1 in 112 have to be overcome, not an easy task for a locomotive just off-shed with its fire not yet burned through.

After a mile of banking the train engine over the gradients known as Camden Bank, the banking engine will drop off allowing it to return to Willesden Shed or further pilot duties at Euston.

A double-headed departure with 'Royal Scot' no. 46128 *The Lovat Scouts* of 5A Crewe North piloted by 'Black 5' no. 44931. The bowler-hatted figure talking to the crew of the 'Black 5' is probably the platform inspector *(D. Loveday)*

The banking engine of the previous page's train is 'Black 5' no. 44904. The engine will give assistance to the train until the top of Camden Bank is reached. *(D. Loveday)*

4

CAMDEN BANK

At the top of Camden Bank on the right of the train lies the large, busy Camden Goods Depot. Many goods trains made their way to London during the night when there was a reduction in line occupation by passenger trains.

The railways had to suffer the legal obligations of The Common Carrier Act until 1962. The act made the railways publish their fixed prices for the carriage of goods traffic, a very unfair situation as road traffic operators could undercut the railway prices and select the more lucrative loads. This left the railways with no choice of what was an economical load. An example of this practice was a road operator delivering packages to one part of the country and leaving the return of empty packages to the railway. As the railway could only charge on a weight basis and had no rights in refusing loads, this was a totally unsatisfactory situation. British Railways figures for 1956 showed 17,600 goods trains per day; this goods traffic was greatly reduced by the advance in road traffic.

Rebuilt 'Patriot' no. 45529 *Stephenson* of 1A Willesden Shed shows a feathering of safety valves as she climbs Camden Bank in June 1963. *(D. Loveday)*

'Duchess' no. 46254 *City of Stoke-on-Trent* powers up Camden Bank with an Up train and is about to pass Camden Shed in June 1963. *(D. Loveday)*

'Black 5' no. 45271, an Armstrong Whitworth-built engine of 1935, catches a glimmer of sunlight as she moves light-engine on the bank in June 1963. (*D. Loveday*)

Armstrong Whitworth-built 'Black 5' no. 45225 of 1935 heads a long train under the footbridge that linked Camden's Goods and Motive Power Depot on 28 February 1959. (*L.G. Marshall/R.S. Collection*)

5

CAMDEN SHED

Camden Motive Power Depot 1B lies directly opposite the goods depot and proves an interesting sight. At the south end of the shed, lines of 'Royal Scot', 'Jubilee' and 'Duchess' class engines are a common sight. These locos have been prepared for future northbound trains in the yard.

On view at the north end of the shed is an array of express engines facing north, all awaiting the time to back down the bank to couple up with their trains in Euston.

Entry to Camden is by the turntable at the north end where engines are turned before proceeding through the shed yard. Passing through the yard, the locos will be watered, fires cleaned under the ash plant and the tenders then topped-up under the coaling stage. Some engines will need boiler wash-outs and others might have their appearance improved by the cleaning gang.

The Camden allocation for 1959 was forty-one locomotives – all essentially express types: four 'Patriot', eight 'Jubilee', nine 'Royal Scot' and eight 'Coronation Pacific' class engines. Twelve 'Jinty' tanks also featured for minor duties. Diesels weren't to arrive until the late 1950s. At the south end of the shed many more engines are on view as they await servicing facilities ready for their next northbound turns of duty.

1B (1948–61).

All coaled up and ready to come off-shed is nicely cleaned no. 46209 *Princess Beatrice* in April 1962. The engine will shortly back down to Euston to couple up to the stock of her train. *(D. Loveday)*

Opposite, bottom: A Glasgow Polmadie-based 66A engine, no. 46222 *Queen Mary*, is being turned ready to enter the servicing facilities at Camden Shed sometime between 1948 and 1950. The engine's livery is of the lined black with maroon and straw lining of the LMS. Although she carries BR numbers, LMS can still be seen on the tender. The early painted version of headboard adorns the smoke-box. *(J. Scott-Morgan/ Lens of Sutton Association)*

Rebuilt 'Royal Scot' no. 46127 *Old Contemptibles* on 28 February 1959. Having arrived at Euston, no. 46127 enters the throat of Camden Shed in order to access the turntable to turn and be serviced ready for its next duty. *(L.G. Marshall/R.S. Collection)*

Under the watchful eye of his driver, the fireman has coupled up the 'Royal Scot' loco no. 46166 *London Rifle Brigade* to the vacuum apparatus to turn the engine ready to enter the shed yard and be coaled up and watered. *(R.S. Collection)*

Opposite, top: A multiple arrival, no. 46234 *Duchess of Abercorn* has turned and follows another member of the class on-shed. *(D. Loveday)*

Opposite, bottom: Class leader no. 46200 *The Princess Royal* of 8A Edge Hill, Liverpool, is coaled up and ready for a return to Liverpool on 12 July 1958. The clutter around the ash pits was a common sight at steam sheds. 'Black 5' no. 45259 of Carlisle Upperby Shed 12B is seen alongside. *(R.S. Collection)*

The unique 8P 'Pacific' no. 71000 *Duke of Gloucester* was a regular visitor to London as the engine spent most of its short life on 'The Mid-Day Scot' turns to and from Crewe. *(D. Loveday)*

The speedometer fitted to some engines in later days is visible on the trailing wheel of rebuilt 'Royal Scot' no. 46127 *Old Contemptibles*. The nameplate is arguably the most ornate of any named locomotive and was much admired. One of the plates can now be seen displayed at the National Railway Museum in York. *(D. Loveday)*

Named by the founder of the Scout movement, Lord Robert Baden-Powell, in December 1930, 'Royal Scot'
no. 46169 carries *The Boy Scout* nameplate. Also on the same date, Lady Baden-Powell named engine
no. 46168 as *The Girl Guide*. Occasionally the two engines were observed on double-headed trains much to
the delight of members of the scouts. *(D. Loveday)*

The nameplate of no. 46169 with the Scouts badge mounted upon the wheel-splasher. *(R.S. Collection)*

Coaled up ready for the road no. 46235 *City of Birmingham* in April 1963, the only member of the class to be officially preserved on withdrawal. The engine now resides in the city of her name. *(D. Loveday)*

'Jubilee' no. 45670 *Prince Rupert* shows limescale staining around the smoke-box in April 1962, a problem more commonly associated with goods engines. These did not receive as much cosmetic attention. *(D. Loveday)*

With two 'Duchesses' also on view, here is Camden's own unique 'Royal Scot' no. 46170 *British Legion* in April 1962. All the locos in this photograph appear to have had attention to their appearance by the cleaners. *(D. Loveday)*

The empty stock of 'The Lakes Express' hauled by 'Black 5' no. 45385 of 3A Bescot Shed emerges from the majestic architecture of Primrose Hill Tunnel. *(Peter Brock Archive/Gresley Society)*

The first of the production run of 'Princess' locomotives, no. (4)6203 *Princess Margaret Rose* is pictured at work during her LMS days at Kilburn. *(R.S. Collection)*

6

WILLESDEN JUNCTION AND LOCO DEPOT

Nearing journey's end, 'The Shamrock', headed by no. 46208 *Princess Helena Victoria*, drifts through a deserted Willesden Junction in 1958. *(R.S. Collection)*

'Royal Scot' no. 46166 *London Rifle Brigade* of 9A Manchester Longsight Shed passes with what is probably 'The Mancunian'. The engine spent the years between 1958 and 1960 at Longsight; during its thirty-four-year lifespan it had forty-four shed locations which makes no. 46166 a candidate for a record number for the class. *(R.S. Collection)*

A grimy no. 46136 *The Border Regiment* passes the Willesden no. 3 signal-box, a typical LNWR design to be seen at many locations. *(R.S. Collection)*

7

WILLESDEN SHED

While 1B Camden Shed serves express passenger engines, the depot at 1A Willesden is mostly concerned with goods train locos. The shed buildings consist of a twelve-road straight shed and a large roundhouse. Willesden's own allocation in 1959 was the largest on the region with 130 locomotives. There were four 'Patriot' and two 'Jubilee' class engines, twenty Fowler 2–6–4 tanks, twenty-seven Fowler 2–6–4 tanks, nine Hughes/Fowler Crab 2–6–0s, six 4F 0–6–0s, nineteen 'Black 5' 4–6–0s, two Ivatt 2–6–0s, seven 'Jinty' 0–6–0 tanks, twenty-seven Stanier 8F 2–8–0s and seven Bowen Cooke 0–8–0s.

The staff at the depot are friendly to enthusiasts, and spotters who venture in will be amazed at the variety of locos on show, many that have made their way into the capital on parcels and goods trains. A look around the shed yard will reveal that Willesden has engines on view that range from the mundane to the magnificent. Among lesser engines it is quite usual to see 'Royal Scot', rebuilt 'Patriot' and the occasional 'Duchess' class engines. Following Camden's closure in 1961, several Stanier 'Pacifics' were transferred to Willesden.

1A (1948–65).

The variety of engines to be found at 1A Willesden Shed can be seen surrounding 4F no. 44451, a 1928 Crewe-built engine, in this photograph from 26 December 1958. A WD 2–8–0 is alongside an LNWR 0–8–0 and behind the 4F is a Fairburn design of tank engine. (*R.S. Collection*)

The Ivatt 2–6–0 design was perpetuated in the BR standard designs. Photographed on 23 November 1963, no. 78019 (now preserved) shows the small detail differences between the two classes. *(R.S. Collection)*

The Ivatt version of 2–6–0 was introduced in late LMS days and proved very popular with enginemen. Seen in April 1963, no. 46517 has cylinder drain cocks open after standing for a period amid the piles of ash by the disposal plant. *(D. Loveday)*

Probably the most successful of all the BR standards were the 9F 2–10–0s. Equally at home on fast freights or express passenger work, these locos ran at speeds of 90mph on several recorded occasions. No. 92156, a 16A Nottingham-based engine, stands at Willesden. (*D. Loveday*)

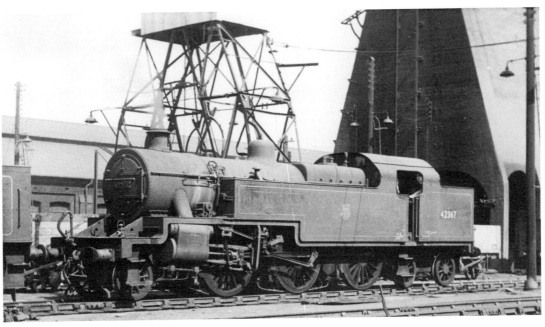

One of Fowler's superb 2–6–4 tank engines, no. 42367, alongside Willesden's coal and ash plants on 20 April 1958. These very popular locos had a handy turn of speed and could run quite well at 80mph. All the class were scrapped, but mystery surrounded no. 42325, which was deliberately crashed for a film in 1962. For years it was rumoured that the loco had been buried where it came to rest, although in 2009 a report of the loco being cut-up on the spot came from a gentleman who had acquired its number plate from the scrap man appeared in a national newspaper. (*R.S. Collection*)

The eye-pleasing lines of a Blackpool-based 'Jubilee', no. 45580 *Burma*, in company with an unidentified Stanier 'Duchess' in April 1963. *(D. Loveday)*

In LMS livery, here is class leader no. (4)5500 '*Patriot*' on 23 April 1939. The engine took over the role of the company's war memorial engine. The subscript of the nameplate reads, 'in memory of the fallen L&NWR employees 1914–1918'. *(R.S. Collection)*

Willesden's own Stanier 2–6–4 tank no. 42431 stands in front of a Fairburn version of the engine on 23 November 1963. The difference can be denoted by the space above the buffer beam on the Fairburn design. *(R.S. Collection)*

'Jinty' 0–6–0 tank engine no. 47501 stands in Willesden Yard on 23 November 1963; the 'UFOs' often seen in pictures of this location are the depot's external lights. *(R.S. Collection)*

8

HARLESDEN TO RUGBY

A wintry scene at Harlesden with no. 46240 *City of Coventry* amid a chilly landscape. *(R.S. Collection)*

The driver of 'Jubilee' no. 45741 *Leinster* peers out at the road ahead; the pleasing appearance of the locomotive shows that the cleaners have done a nice job. *(R.S. Collection)*

The 'Princess' at speed at Hatch End is no. 46205 *Princess Victoria* with a lengthy express. The extra rails needed for electric trains are on the right of the view. *(R.S. Collection)*

Underneath the arches at Bushey, no. 46206 *Princess Marie Louise* roars over the water pick-up troughs in about 1961. This is the first of nine troughs between Euston and Carlisle. *(6201 Princess Elizabeth Society)*

'Royal Scot' no. 46119 *Lancashire Fusilier* storms through Watford Junction station, its tender showing the early BR logo. The advertisement for Palethorpes Sausages is displayed on the loco shed wall. This, together with one for Virol, was seen at many stations. *(R.S. Collection)*

The driver of LMS liveried no. (4)2489, built at Derby in 1937, is about to climb on board his charge. The Stanier 2–6–4 tank engines numbered 206 in total, proved excellent performers and could produce a good turn of speed; they could be regarded as a tank version of the 'Black 5s'. *(Gresley Society)*

A high elevation view of rebuilt 'Patriot' no. 45526 *Morecambe and Heysham* at the head of an express.
The loco shed of Watford 1C is on the right-hand side; its largest allocation of engines were always 2–6–4T
types. *(R.S. Collection)*

'Jubilee' no. 45726 *Vindictive*, coupled to a small Fowler type tender, enters Watford on 6 December 1956.
(R. Coggan/R.S. Collection)

Princess Victoria no. 46205 passes Kings Langley signal-box with 'The Merseyside Express'. The engine carries an experimentally modified motion bracket, which was different to the rest of the class. *(R.S. Collection)*

A double-header of a 2P 4–4–0 no. 425 and an unidentified 'Jubilee' with a Down express at Apsley on 18 August 1939, an LMS scene shortly before the outbreak of war. *(H.C. Doyle/Gresley Society)*

An Up Northampton to Tring train on 16 July 1939, headed by 2P 4–4–0 no. 1113. The exchange apparatus for the postal special and postman's hut are seen at trackside. *(H.C. Doyle/Gresley Society)*

Rebuilt 'Patriot' no. 45540 *Sir Robert Turnbull* wears a 21A Saltley shedplate on 17 March 1962. Passing through Bletchley with a train of just two coaches, this could be just a shunting movement, as the two lamps on the loco appear to be two different aspects, denoting a shunter. *(R.S. Collection)*

One of the 'Patriot' class engines to remain in original condition, Crewe North 5A-based unnamed no. 45544 is at the head of a lengthy express on 8 August 1959. A variety of lineside buildings at Bletchley typical of the steam age are on the left and on the right is a very tall signal post evident at many locations. *(R.S. Collection)*

The Up 'Royal Scot' headed by no. 46249 *City of Sheffield* passes by Loughton Sidings – now the site of Milton Keynes station – on 20 June 1953. *(G.W. Goslin)*

Opposite, bottom: 'Black 5' no. 45388 stands outside her home shed 1E (1952–65) Bletchley. The loco had probably been returned after an overhaul and being painted in unlined black livery. Enthusiasts sometimes scraped off the paint with a coin when nobody was looking to reveal the original red and grey lining. *(R.S. Collection)*

'Jubilee' no. 45569 *Fisher* passes Blisworth signal-box on 16 June 1951 with an Up express. The tall signal post is typical of many found on the line where the driver's view was obscured by bridges and station buildings. The water column is of the standard LNWR variety. *(G.W. Goslin)*

'Patriot' no. (4)5543 *Home Guard* is captured at Kilsby at 5.32 p.m. on 19 July 1938 with a Down Liverpool train. *(Gresley Society)*

9

RUGBY MIDLAND TO STAFFORD

Rebuilt 'Royal Scot' no. (4)6129 *The Scottish Horse* starts out of Rugby Midland. Some opinions say this is the most pleasing one with no smoke deflectors on the loco – rebuilds would all eventually receive smoke deflectors. *(R.S. Collection)*

For comparison, a 'Royal Scot' in original condition, no. (4)6139 *The Welch Regiment*, in the same location. Opinions varied as to which design looked the best. All the 'Royal Scot' class engines would be rebuilt into taper boiler versions, the last being no. 46137 in 1955. *(R.S. Collection)*

Relegated to a parcels train no. 46248 *City of Leeds* shows she is in good condition with safety valves feathering. The LNWR-style water column has heating provided by the fire basket complete with a generous amount of coal. The date is December 1961. *(Gordon Coltas)*

Passing Rugby no. 2 signal-box with 'The Mancunian' is 'Royal Scot' no. 46116 *Irish Guardsman* in 1953. (*Gordon Coltas*)

Former streamlined no. 46248 *City of Leeds* passes through Nuneaton's Trent Valley station. The loco was for a short time named *King George VI* until no. 46244 received the nameplate and identity. (*R.S. Collection*)

The Trent Valley

The stations along the Trent Valley prove a rich picking ground for the enthusiasts who gather on platforms along the route. One station that actively forbids spotters is the most advantageous of all, Tamworth. Shortly after nationalisation, acts of vandalism to railway equipment (almost unheard of for the time) forced the prohibition of trainspotting at several stations. Not to be deterred, the spotters still arrive in large numbers at Tamworth, but now gather in a field just outside the station. With a long, clear view of four lines and four signals that announce the arrival of expresses on the WCML, enthusiasm often reaches fever pitch. 'Semis', 'Lizzies', 'Scots', 'Jubs' and 'Pats' roar by at speeds of 80mph or more. Such is the frequency of trains that in just a two-hour period it is normal to witness well over twenty different expresses each headed by 'namers'. An added bonus of Tamworth is the High Level line, which crosses over the Low Level. Normally around ten trains pass over these lines in the same two-hour period. The engines on the High Level are not top-drawer for spotters; the occasional 'Jubilee' appearing among a variety that ranges from 'Black 5s', 8Fs, BR standard class 5 4–6–0s, Hughes/Fowler Crabs and 'Spaceships' – the BR 2–10–0s.

'Royal Scot' no. 46135 *The East Lancashire Regiment* passing the lineside water tower by Tamworth Low Level station. *(R.S. Collection)*

Opposite, bottom: All appears to be going well for 'Royal Scot' no. 46169 *The Boy Scout,* as the fireman has a break from shovelling coal to gaze out of his side of the cab. *(R.S. Collection)*

Princess Helena Victoria no. 46208 passes under a signal gantry. On the left is a fog man's hut and apparatus, used to place detonators on the line. The fogs that once blighted the country are now history, thanks to the Clean Air Act of 1956. *(R.S. Collection)*

'Royal Scot' no. 46101 *Royal Scots Grey* passes through Lichfield with 'The Lakes Express' on 7 July 1962. The loco is one of several which were rather camera shy. (*A. Sullivan/R.S. Collection*)

Opposite, top: A rebuilt 'Patriot', no. 45529 *Stephenson*, leaves a trail of exhaust while running through Lichfield Trent Valley at speed. The two colours of the coaching stock and the early tender BR logo date the scene to the early 1950s. (*R.S. Collection*)

Opposite, bottom: Hughes/Fowler Crab 2–6–0 no. 42848 hurries through Tamworth on a cold winter's day. The Crabs were very powerful locos and popular with enginemen, except for disposal, when its long fire-bars and smokebox lugs prompted a few adverse comments. (*J. Burrows/Gresley Society*)

The popular 7F locos were no strangers to the WCML. Sizeable allocations were based at Rugby, Nuneaton, Bletchley and Willesden for use on goods trains. After years of open-air preservation (neglect), no. 49395 has been restored and is now in superb working condition. *(R.S. Collection)*

Heavily loaded, 'The Mid-Day Scot' is causing no. 46209 *Princess Beatrice* to work hard through the Trent Valley, as the exhaust shows. *(Travel Lens Photographic)*

10

STAFFORD TO CREWE

A Down express on 3 June 1952, ex-streamlined no. 46246 *City of Manchester* has the sloping firebox appearance that earned the nickname 'Semis' from spotters. It would be 1960 before it became the last member of the class to receive a fully rounded smokebox. Stafford station was rebuilt to accommodate the electric era. *(E.R. Morton/R.S. Collection)*

The last built 'Black 5', no. 44687 allocated to 9A Longsight entering Stafford station on 3 June 1952, was a Horwich Works product. With double chimney, high running plate and Caprotti valve gear this engine, together with no. 44686, were unique members of the 842 'Black 5s'. *(E.R. Morton/R.S. Collection)*

A Saltley 21A-based 4F 0–6–0, no. 44226 heads a Birmingham–Stafford goods train in 1962. The 4F was always a subject of love/hate, although if they were really as bad as stated, would the Midland Railway and LMS really have built 772 examples between 1911 and 1941? *(R.S. Collection)*

Built by the North British Loco Works in 1935, 'Jubilee' no. 45604 *Ceylon* has simmering safety valves. This shows all is well with steam pressure as she starts her train out of Stafford on 15 March 1959. The signal gantry would fall victim to the line's electrification in the 1960s. *(H.K. Boulter/Ted Hancock)*

City of Liverpool no. 46247 heads 'The Royal Scot' through Stafford station on 3 June 1952. The chamfered smokebox shows the loco is a former streamliner; a fully rounded version was fitted in May 1958. Yet again the advertisements for Palethorpes Sausages and Virol appear on railway property. *(E.R. Morton/R.S. Collection)*

Pictured against the 5C coaling plant is class leader no. 45500 *Patriot* on-shed, 15 March 1959. The circular wheel centres are evidence of the engine having former 'Claughton' class wheels, probably the only old parts in the so-called rebuild of the engine. In the background a 'Jubilee' passes through Stafford station. *(H.K. Boulter/Ted Hancock)*

Opposite, top: The driver of 'Black 5' no. 45288 spots the photographer as his engine rounds the curve at Stafford with a freight train in March 1963. The engine was allocated to 1A Willesden Shed. *(R.S. Collection)*

Opposite, bottom: In somewhat grimy BR lined-black livery on 30 July 1956, Compound 4–4–0 no. 41060 is far removed from the days when the class were nicknamed Crimson Ramblers by the Midland Railway. Like many classmates, no. 41060 was an early candidate for withdrawal. *(R.S. Collection)*

11

AROUND CREWE

A 'Duchess' in the heyday of the streamlined age, no. 46224 *Princess Alexandra* replenishes its tender from the troughs at Whitmore at 3.43 p.m. on 28 July 1938. *(Gresley Society)*

The Down 'Mid-Day Scot' headed by no. 46209 *Princess Beatrice* approaches Whitmore on 23 July 1955. The early BR tender logo confirms the date of the scene. *(E.R. Morton/ R.S. Collection)*

Relegated to a parcels train, no. 46221 *Queen Elizabeth* has a clear exhaust and lifting safety valves as she passes a goods train. With the unreliability problems of early diesels, the wisdom of demoting 'Duchess' class engines onto lesser duties was questionable. *(R.S. Collection)*

'Black 5' no. 45037 heads a ten-coach express under the gantries for the electric services in 1963. The engine was a 1934/5 build from Vulcan Foundry, Crewe. *(R.S. Collection)*

12

CREWE STATION

As a train entered the station the articulate tones of the station announcer informed passengers that, 'This is Crewe, Crewe station.' For the young boys on board the train, they already knew. The window of the carriage was wound down in order to open the door and exit the train quickly, for not a minute's spotting could be lost on a trip to Crewe! The spot favoured by most was the lattice bridge which spanned platforms at the north end of the station. Every weekend and during school holidays hundreds of boys would descend onto the station for what many will now recall as perfect days.

If the crowds of spotters did not allow space on the bridge, then a decision had to be made of which platform end to occupy. Preparation for the day started at home by emptying school satchels, replacing the schoolbooks with rations for the duration. Crisps (with the little blue bag of salt), jam butties, a bottle of Jusoda or Tizer pop and essentials such as paper, pencil and *Ian Allan Spotters abc* all went in. Few spotters carried cameras, as equipment of the day was the box camera which, with the problem of composing a picture from the inverted image, only allowed eight or twelve photographs. Fortunately adult photographers were there to record the scene. By the late 1950s the Brownie 127 camera became available with the result that school camera clubs would see an increase in membership.

As a train came into sight, excited cries of 'Semi', 'Lizzy', 'Scot', 'Pat' or 'Jub' would be heard. The 'Semis' would raise a cheer and the 'Lizzys' produced an ecstatic response, as they were few in number. 'Black 5s' were numerous, although the four named examples of the class proved elusive to many. The shout of 'scrap it' greeted some engines due to the spotter having seen it on many occasions; how they now wish that those words could be retracted had they realised the rapid demise of steam engines. So busy was the scene that a fresh sighting every three minutes or so could be made. When hurried visits to the gents' toilets were made, it was at the risk of missing that elusive engine you wished to see. Not only were there passenger train departures and arrivals, but numerous light-engine movements. These would be to and from Crewe North shed; sometimes several coupled together would be en route to the works. At Crewe the station pilots, 'Jinty' tanks and 2P 4–4–0s, would periodically appear from hiding to remove or add stock to a train.

Many spotters would hover around an engine, peering into the cab, and make a polite request to climb aboard – in most cases they were refused permission. Occasionally a goods train came through the station; its engine, one of the lesser breeds, would not attract much attention. Goods trains had their own lines that reduced congestion in the station by using the avoiding lines that burrowed for 2 miles underground by Crewe South loco shed. Even with declining freight traffic it produced around 38,000 wagons in the 1950s. Dealing with goods traffic were the huge marshalling yards of Basford Hall, situated at the south end of Crewe, and around 120 engines of 5B Crewe South loco shed. A day's loco spotting was very rewarding but dirty; hair would change to a darker shade and soot deposits blackened faces. Happy days!

A 'Royal Scot' and a 'Patriot', both in original condition during early BR days, on 26 February 1950. The 'Patriot' is no. 45548 *Lytham St Annes* and the 'Royal Scot' no. 46140 *The Kings Royal Rifle Corps*. The 'Royal Scot' would be rebuilt in May 1952 as a taper boiler engine. *(J. Ward/R.S. Collection)*

'Royal Scot' no. 46139 *The Welch Regiment* awaits the signal to head north in 1952. The lighting post to the left appears to have someone doing maintenance. Had it been a spotter, they would soon have attracted the attention of the Railway Police! *(J. Neve/R.S. Collection)*

A double-header with 'Royal Scot' no. 46166 *London Rifle Brigade* leading an unidentified Stanier loco, attracts the attention of the spotters on the north end footbridge. *(R.S. Collection)*

An unnamed member of the 'Patriot' class, no. 45544 of 8A Liverpool Edge Hill Shed is awaiting the whistle to get her train moving in May 1959. All carriage doors are secured ready for departure. *(R.S. Collection)*

Fowler 4F 0–6–0 no. 44450 unusually takes some goods stock through Crewe on 8 August 1962. Normally goods traffic uses the avoiding lines, nicknamed the 'Muck hole'. *(R.S. Collection)*

Vulcan Foundry-built 'Black 5' no. 45044 (seen here on 6 August 1953) of the 1934/5 batches with combined top-feed and dome, departs at the south end of Crewe station. The wind shelter is an LNWR construction which can be seen at several other station locations. *(R.S. Collection)*

The fireman of 'Royal Scot' no. 46141 *The North Staffordshire Regiment* climbs back on board after presumably checking some details with control. The large box on the running plate is for the sanding gear. *(R.S. Collection)*

A close-up of no. 46141's nameplate – the badge gave the North Staffordshire Railway its nickname of the 'Knotty'. *(R.S. Collection)*

Time for a chat between the crew of 'Black 5' no. 45009 and the station porters in a quiet moment as the engine awaits the right away. A possible topic of conversation could be the performance of the town's football team, Crewe Alexandra. *(R.S. Collection)*

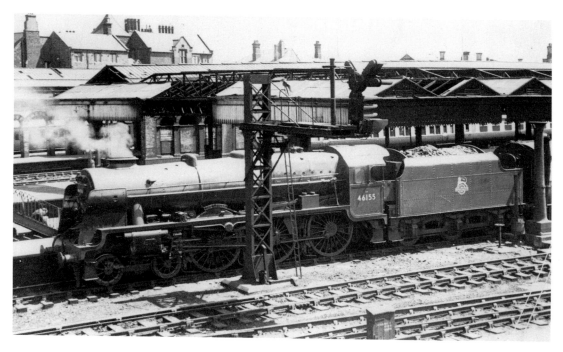

There are plenty of spotters on the footbridge to witness 'Patriot' no. 45546 *Fleetwood* as she immerses them in steam from her safety valves. *(R.S. Collection)*

Opposite, top: Red liveried no. 46207 curiously named *Princess Arthur of Connaught* – which causes spotters the confusion of how a Princess can have a man's name – in 1957. *(R. Harding/R.S. Collection)*

Opposite, bottom: Some of the architecture of Crewe is in the background of this photograph of 'Royal Scot' no. 46155 *The Lancer* on a near-deserted Crewe station. *(R.S. Collection)*

Sporting the tartan version of the headboard, no. 46244 *King George VI* of 1B Camden Shed has charge of 'The Royal Scot'. Passing through the station on the right of this photograph is an engineers' train with the Crewe Breakdown Crane. *(R.S. Collection)*

Opposite, top: Running through light-engine, the long-time Crewe-allocated 'Jubilee' no. 45666 *Cornwallis* is pictured on 9 May 1960. *(R.S. Collection)*

Opposite, bottom: So large are the LMS 'Pacifics' that it is difficult to obtain a side view. The pleasing lines of no. 46209 *Princess Beatrice* are captured on a Crewe departure on 9 May 1960. *(R.S. Collection)*

An immaculately cleaned no. 46254 *City of Stoke-on-Trent* lingers under the Crewe north end footbridge.
A few spotters on the bridge are busily recording engine numbers. The loco is one of only four in the class
to have a badge above the nameplate. *(R.S. Collection)*

Opposite, top: With an array of express power always on show, the sight of a goods loco does not attract
much attention from spotters. Fowler 4F 0–6–0 no. 44432 drifts by on 9 May 1960. The loco is fitted with the
tender cab to be found on only a few 4Fs. *(R.S. Collection)*

Opposite, bottom: One of the 'Duchess' class engines favoured by a repaint into lined red livery, long-term 1B
Camden-based no. 46240 *City of Coventry* is about to depart from Crewe. *(R.S. Collection)*

13

JUNCTIONS AROUND CREWE

Although not on the WCML, Shrewsbury is the destination for many of the locos that have been overhauled at Crewe Works. After emerging from the works looking as-new with sparkling paintwork, the relatively short trips to Shrewsbury bring great delight to local spotters as many rarities can be noted.

This testing makes good sense; freshly fitted bearings can bed in and be checked before the engine is released back into traffic with its home depot.

The station, a Tudor Gothic building which resembles a university, is a distinguished piece of architecture which blends well with the town's other stylish buildings. Unfortunately its roof was removed, which took away part of the station's character.

Rebuilt 'Royal Scot' no. 46120 *Royal Inniskilling Fusilier* of 9A Manchester Longsight Shed blows steam as she awaits departure. The engine's cabside numbers are in the style of early BR livery. (*R.S. Collection*)

Chester Midland 6A-based no. 46124 *London Scottish* departs Shrewsbury with an ordinary passenger train, probably an ex-works test run from Crewe. *(R.S. Collection)*

In original as-built form, 'Patriot' no. 45538 *Giggleswick* rounds the curve to exit Shrewsbury station. The loco's name puzzles spotters, for it is that of a public school in the north of England. *(R.S. Collection)*

The Route from Crewe to Liverpool Lime Street

Crewe 158 miles from London Euston
Weaver Junction signal-box 174 miles
Runcorn 181 miles
Allerton 188 miles
West Allerton 189 miles
Mossley Hill 189
Sefton Park 190 miles
Edge Hill 192 miles
Liverpool Lime Street 193 miles

The 'Princess' class engines of 8A Edge Hill Shed were the preferred motive power for the services to Liverpool. The most important named train, 'The Merseyside Express', was a non-stop run of nearly four hours. 'The Red Rose' (introduced in 1951 to celebrate the Festival of Britain) had just one stop. Both heavily loaded trains always require much hard work by footplate crews.

Often the subject of ill-founded comments, the unique no. 6202 *Turbomotive* was used very successfully on Liverpool trains. The locomotive, which produced no hammer blow to the track, was never really opened up to its full potential. Sadly no. 6202 gained a reputation for poor reliability owing to the nature of specialist replacement parts during the Second World War. Rebuilt as the ill-fated no. 46202 *Princess Anne*, it was badly damaged in the Harrow & Wealdstone disaster and scrapped shortly afterwards.

The Route from Crewe to Holyhead

Crewe 158 miles from London Euston
Tattenhall Junction 172 miles
Chester 179 miles
Saltney Junction 181 miles
Connah's Quay 188 miles
Holywell Junction 196 miles
Prestatyn 205 miles
Rhyl 209 miles
Colwyn Bay 219 miles
Llandudno Junction 223 miles
Bangor 239 miles
Gaerwen 245 miles
Rhosneigr 256 miles
Holyhead 263 miles from London Euston

The line to North Wales via Chester is the route of the oldest named express, that being 'The Irish Mail', and is generally regarded as being one of the easier routes on the system as it does not have any severe gradients. The destination of 'The Irish Mail' is the port of Holyhead for the sailings to Dun Laoghaire.

Livestock trains from Ireland provided the railway with much traffic. At times these trains had to be delayed after the sea crossing if the animals are not considered fit to travel after examination by a vet.

The other named express, 'The Welshman', follows the same route as 'The Irish Mail' to reach its destinations of Portmadoc and Pwllheli.

The new 'Britannia' class engines were for a time used on the North Wales expresses, but the preferred engines soon returned in the shape the rebuilt 'Royal Scot' class – in the latter days of steam, Stanier 'Pacifics' could be seen.

The holiday period brought many trains of visitors to the North Wales coast to enjoy the sun in places such as Rhyl and Llandudno.

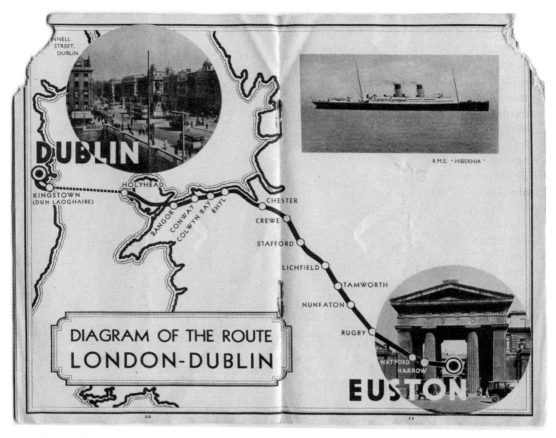

Map detail of the route of 'The Irish Mail' from the LMS publication, *The Story of the Irish Mail 1848–1934*.

The Route from Crewe to Manchester London Road

Crewe 158 miles from London Euston
Sandbach 162 miles
Holme Chapel 166 miles
Goosetrey 168 miles
Chelford 172 miles
Alderley Edge 175 miles
Wilmslow 177 miles
Styal 178 miles
Heald Green 180 miles
Gatley 181 miles
Burnage 184 miles
Cheadle Hulme 180 miles
Stockport 183 miles
Heaton Chapel 184 miles
Levenshulme 186 miles
Longsight 187 miles
Manchester London Road 188.9 miles

(Some expresses travelled via Stoke-on-Trent having left the main line at Colwich. The overall distance on this route is some 5½ miles shorter than that of Crewe–Stockport routed trains.)

The Manchester trains of the 'The Mancunian' and 'The Lancastrian' are workings from Manchester's Longsight Shed 9A. The variety of engines feature 'Royal Scot', 'Patriot', 'Jubilee' and 'Britannia' classes nos 70031–70032–70033–70043. Rumour among London Road spotters was of a Saturday afternoon arrival by a Stanier 'Pacific' (a rarity to the area); this proved to be true on several occasions.

14

CREWE SHED AND WORKS

Formerly of 5E Alsager Shed, the W12 plate and lack of shedplate show that Fowler 4F 0–6–0 no. 44405 is on Crewe Works shunter duties. *(D. Barton/R.S. Collection)*

Pictured above the inspection pits in July 1963, Yorkshire-based 'Jubilee' no. 45695 *Minotaur* is a credit to her home shed's cleaners. *(Gresley Society)*

'Royal Scot' no. 46104 *Scottish Borderer* is in light steam outside the works along with another member of the class. *(R.S. Collection)*

Inside the roundhouse at Crewe North is Camden 1B-based no. 46209 *Princess Beatrice* alongside 'Royal Scot' no. 46110 *Grenadier Guardsman*. *(6201 Princess Elizabeth Society)*

The unique BR 'Pacific' no. 71000 *Duke of Gloucester* shows its stylish lines at Crewe North Shed. For many years its appearance was overshadowed by being a poor performer. *(R.S. Collection)*

Formerly 6G Llandudno Junction-based, the W12 plate shows that Fowler 4F 0–6–0 no. 44525 was on Crewe Works shunter duties when this photograph was taken on 20 June 1965. *(R.S. Collection)*

The Yellow Stripes Origin

With the planned electrification of lines to the south of Crewe, limited clearances between the top of locos and the new overhead catenary wires were foreseen as future dangers to footplate crews once the wires were energised.

A detailed study took place during the early 1960s in the Derby Works Drawing Office of drawing ref. DD5014. From the data, a list of locomotives which measured over 13ft 1in from rail level to chimney top was prepared. All those identified had a 6in diagonal yellow stripe painted on cab sides; some also received similar treatment in error. After the stripe was applied, the locomotives were then banned from working south of Crewe when the electrification became live.

Another consequence of electrification was the position of the top lamp brackets on smokebox fronts; many engines had these moved to lower and slightly off-centre position. The list of locos to which the yellow stripe was applied, which is as comprehensive as photographic evidence has so far produced, is:

4F 0–6–0	44431	45601	45704
43893	44441	45604	45705
43906	44446	45608	45721
43913	44450	45617	45723
43940	44458	45621	45735
43967	44484	45626	45736
43968	44525	45627	45739
43999	44580	45629	45742
44023	44593	45631	
44056		45632	'Royal Scot' 4–6–0
44057	'Jubilee' 4–6–0	45633	46115
44075	45562	45641	46122
44113	45563	45642	46128
44125	45565	45643	46140
44149	45567	45647	46148
44181	45573	45654	46152
44218	45574	45655	46155
44243	45581	45657	46160
44250	45583	45660	46165
44260	45584	45661	46166
44462	45586	45672	
44263	45588	45674	
44276	45590	45675	
44278	45593	45676	
44294	45595	45684	
44373	45596	45694	
44400	45597	45697	
44401	45598	45699	
44414	45600	45703	

'Duchess' 4–6–2	46249	G2 0–8–0	8F 2–8–0
46225	46250	48895	48688
46226	46254	49078	48700
46228	46255	49173	48773
46237	46256	49340	
46238	46257	49361	'Clan' 4–6–2
46239		49407	72006
46240		49430	
46241			WD Austerity
46243			2–8–0
46244			90125
46245			90261
46248			90466

Crewe Works Open Days

For many years, the event eagerly awaited by both young and old enthusiasts was Crewe Works Open Day. Staged over two days, open days attracted crowds of thousands of visitors. The chance to see locomotives passing through the works was one attraction. Among those hoped-for sightings were elusive engines from the Scottish Region; the 'Duchess', 'Jubilee', 'Princess' and 'Royal Scot' classes, which rarely seemed to venture into England.

The lifting of an engine by the overhead cranes inside the works was always something worth seeing as well as those sparkling with new paintwork after general overhaul. On view would be brand new engines ready to enter service and also lines of those awaiting their fate in the scrap lines. The chances of sighting a rarity before its demise proved very popular even though its appearance would be far from the pristine condition of other locos on show.

As if the sound of steam locomotives simmering and whistling were not enough, a brass band would provide musical entertainment throughout the event. The Webb Crewe Works Charity Fund administered and distributed proceeds from the open days to various worthwhile charity recipients. On the weekend of 10 and 11 September 2005 what was probably the last Open Weekend took place. The site is now privately owned by Bombardier Transportation who kindly allowed the event called the 'Great Gathering' to take place. Sponsors included Jessops, Mortons, Hornby and *Heritage Railway* magazine. Over the two days an attendance of over 45,000 people witnessed a truly great spectacle and raised around £250,000 for charities. The majority of steam exhibits were no longer part of British Railways but those of preservation societies whose members had raised funds to purchase the majority of the locos from the scrapyard.

Possibly for the last time ever, the selection of locomotives included steam, diesel and electric and catered for all tastes with the big four's steam fleets well represented; from the GWR two 'Hall' class locos and a 'Manor' while the Southern had only one loco on view, a West Country 'Pacific'. The LNER had an A4, a B1 and the legendary *Flying Scotsman*, although the LMS exhibits proved the highlight of the event with four Stanier 'Pacifics', a 'Jubilee', a 'Black 5', an 8F, a Stanier 2–6–0 and an Ivatt 2–6–0. From BR there were three different locos, *Duke of Gloucester*, a standard 2–6–4 tank and a 9F. As could be expected, diesel and electric forms of traction made up the majority of exhibits on show.

The scene the 'Pacifics' represented could have been that of London's 1B Camden Shed in the 1950s as all had been regular visitors to the capital. All five 'Pacifics' have a charmed existence as none were officially preserved. Purchased by Sir Billy Butlin for attractions to display at his holiday camps were no. 46233 *Duchess of Sutherland*, no. 46229 *Duchess of Hamilton* and no. 46203 *Princess Margaret Rose*. It was to be some years before they were purchased for preservation and only then did no. 46229 become part of the National Railway Museum Collection. No. 46201 *Princess Elizabeth* was the only loco to be purchased directly from BR after withdrawal by the society that bears her name. For no. 46229 *Duchess of Hamilton* this was to be its last event before being taken away to emerge as a streamliner once more, a complete reversal to her original as-built appearance.

Much thought had gone into the display of 'Pacific' power. Perfectly positioned for photography on what will probably be the only occasion were four Stanier 'Pacifics': no. (4)6201 *Princess Elizabeth*, no. 46203 *Princess Margaret Rose*, no. 46233 *Duchess of Sutherland* and no. 46229 *Duchess of Hamilton*. They are together with BR 71000 *Duke of Gloucester*. Three are seen standing as in days gone by, waiting to head the crack express trains they were designed for.

A little licence had been taken with no. 46203 *Princess Margaret Rose,* as 'The Caledonian' headboard was only once carried by a 'Princess' – on 17 August 1960 by no. 46211 *Queen Maud.*

15

TO LIVERPOOL

The class of locomotive that is sadly missed by enthusiasts is the 'Patriot' in unrebuilt condition. The ones that avoided being rebuilt were:

45500 *Patriot*
45501 *St. Dunstan's*
45502
45503 *The Royal Leicestershire Regiment*
45504 *Royal Signals*
45505 *The Royal Ordnance Corps*
45506 *The Royal Pioneer Corps*
45507
45508
45509 *Derbyshire Yeomanry*
45510
45511 *Isle of Man*
45513
45515 *Caernarvon*
45516 *The Bedfordshire and Hertfordshire Regiment*
45517
45518 *Bradshaw*

45519 *Lady Godiva*
45520 *Llandudno*
45524 *Blackpool*
45533 *Lord Rathmore*
45537 *Private E. Sykes*
45538 *Giggleswick*
45539 *E.C. Trench*
45541 *Duke of Sutherland*
45542
45543 *Home Guard*
45544
45546 *Fleetwood*
45547
45548 *Lytham St Annes*
45549
45550
45551

Of the 'Patriot' class engines only one had its appearance marred. This was no. 45508, which had been fitted with a stovepipe chimney, more fitting to a lineside hut than a locomotive. All the class were withdrawn and scrapped.

A sight that would delight spotters as a 'Patriot' races by in full cry past a heavy goods train of track panels. Unrebuilt no. 45513 was one of several within the class never to receive a name.
(R.S. Collection)

Standing at Liverpool Lime Street, 'Black 5' no. 44772, a Horwich-built engine from 1950, was one of the batch to receive Skefco roller bearings. The photograph dates from 14 May 1956. The forward-mounted top-feed was an indication of the later built 'Black 5s'. (*J. Peden/R.S. Collection*)

Workmen have a rest and watch activities around the preparation for departure of 'The Merseyside Express' with a dirty no. 46200 *The Princess Royal* in charge, *c.* 1952. The coach end boards and the ancient lorry are amid the platform clutter. (*J. Peden/R.S. Collection*)

'Black 5' no. 45242, an Armstrong Whitworth engine of 1936–8, was one of the first batch to receive the separate top-feed and dome which then became standard. *(B. Taylor/R.S. Collection)*

Reflective glows of the station lighting indicate how dull the interior of Lime Street is, as 'Black 5' no. 44906 awaits departure. *(B. Taylor/R.S. Collection)*

The arched roof of Lime Street shows in the background as 'Black 5' no. 44711 heads a parcels train. *(B. Taylor/R.S. Collection)*

The power of 'Royal Scot' no. 46114 *Coldstream Guardsman* is captured as she eases her train away from Lime Street station. The smokebox shows signs of charring.
(*R.S. Collection*)

Factory chimneys, lamps, signals and a glimpse of Edge Hill's gridiron surround Super D no. 49224 heading a goods train on 30 April 1957. *(B. Taylor/R.S. Collection)*

Edge Hill Shed (1948–68).

Fowler class 4F no. 44587 is coupled to what appears to be a high-sided tender, some of which were fitted to 'Jubilee' class engines when new but were short-lived with the class. *(D. Loveday)*

'Royal Scot' no. 46119 *Lancashire Fusilier* is coaled up ready for departure off Edge Hill Shed. *(D. Loveday)*

On shed at 8A Edge Hill are two 'Princesses', no. 46208 *Princess Helena Victoria* and no. 46204 *Princess Louise*. Both locos were withdrawn from service in October 1962. As shedplates have been removed and buffers greased, they are stored out of use. *(D. Loveday)*

Opposite, top: Very much an old LNWR design, Super D no. 49173 shows the H spoke design of driving wheel familiar with LNWR locomotives. The Super Ds wheezed along and gave the impression of struggling with a load; this, though, was the normal sound of the engine as they wheezed even when running light-engine. *(D. Loveday)*

Opposite, bottom: 'Patriot' no. 45543 *Home Guard* on shed at 8A. The loco was destined to head the last 'Patriot' working, in October 1962. *(D. Loveday)*

In the grimy condition that would become normal in the late 1960s, 'Black 5' no. 44866 awaits the the signal for departure from Liverpool's Edge Hill station on 3 September 1966. *(B. Taylor/R.S. Collection)*

16

PRESTON TO CARNFORTH

Although Preston is overlooked as a stop for Anglo-Scottish services, it is, nevertheless, a large station which handles local traffic to Blackburn, Burnley, Manchester, Ormskirk and Colne. As well as Liverpool, Barrow-in-Furness and Blackpool, all these destinations are ex-Lancashire and Yorkshire Railway routes. The Blackpool trains that pass through bring in hundreds of thousands of visitors and produce a large variety of motive power at peak holiday periods.

Confusion can happen at Preston station for passengers travelling to the Fylde Coast from the north. The train passes through in one direction and some ten minutes later passes through Preston once again but in the other direction, this owing to there being no link to the west side. A change in direction is made by using the loop at the south end of Preston known as Farrington Curve.

After a fire which occurred in 1960, 10B was merely a roofless storage area; in this photograph two 'Patriot' class engines, no. 45543 *Home Guard* and no. 45550, have chimneys covered and await their fate. Other locos would soon gather on the site but both these 'Patriot' engines succumbed to the cutter's torch in 1963. (*Vic Nutton/Travel Lens Photographic*)

The signal-boxes around Preston are large LNWR style and control the impressive signal gantries that spread across the lines. The Preston Motive Power depot 10B (24K from 1958 to 1961), situated to the north of the station, is a nine-track structure with an allocation of around thirty engines. A few unrebuilt 'Patriot' class engines, a 'Jubilee' and 'Black 5s' are the express types shedded here.

In June 1960, the shed at Preston caught fire causing severe damage to the building and also to some locos inside the shed. Among the casualties were Hughes/Fowler Crab no. 42707, BR 2–6–0 no. 78037 and two 7F 0–8–0 engines, nos 49104 and 49382.

The now-preserved no. 46233 *Duchess of Sutherland* pauses at Preston with 'The Mid-Day Scot' and is noted by the gabardine-coated schoolboys enjoying a day's spotting. *(R.S. Collection)*

Opposite, top: The driver of rebuilt 'Patriot' no. 45531 *Sir Frederick Harrison* is about to make some smoke of his own as he waits for the signals to clear. *(R.S. Collection)*

Opposite, bottom: 'Royal Scot' no. 46166 *London Rifle Brigade*, seen here in 1963, was built at Derby in 1930 for £6,467 and withdrawn in 1964 after about two million miles of service. *(R.S. Collection)*

By Train to the Seaside

With the introduction of paid holidays, whole industries in towns would close down for a week in what was known as Wakes Weeks. During the winter months seaside towns advertised the merits of their resorts with the familiar posters of bathing beauties posing with a beach ball on a golden beach. When the day arrived for the holiday it was not unusual to see hundreds of holidaymakers queueing on station platforms awaiting the train. Youngsters would worry if there would be enough room for everyone on the train and wonder if the engine to transport them would be a 'Duchess'. The youngsters in many instances would be disappointed when a 4F, a Crab or, in some instances, a WD 2–8–0 drew the train in. Such were the demands on the railway operating departments that anything and everything sometimes had to be used. For those who could not afford or did not want a week away from home, weekday excursions featured many destinations at very modest prices.

'There's a famous seaside town called Blackpool, that's noted for fresh air and fun,' the opening words of the monologue performed by comedy actor Stanley Holloway described the popularity of Blackpool on the Fylde Coast. Other resorts such as Morecambe and Southport as well as those in North Wales were also very popular but none compared to Blackpool. The three stations and nearly 4 miles of sidings show just how vast the invasions of tourists could be.

Met at stations by the local boys with their trucks made from old boxes and pram wheels, they offered, for a small charge, to take holidaymakers' suitcases to their accommodation, normally one of the hundreds of terraced houses that abound in the resort. The attractions of Blackpool featured the 'Golden Mile' filled with catchpenny entertainments, fish and chips, rock shops, joke shops, amusement arcades and the trams. Not to be forgotten are the miles of (then) golden sand, donkey rides, deck chairs and the compulsory dip in the sea, plus sandcastles for the youngsters with newly purchased buckets and spades. These were the days of woollen bathing trunks which when wet proved most uncomfortable and would loosen with embarrassing results.

In the 1950s, late in the season, very popular for visitors was a visit to Bloomfield Road to watch Blackpool FC's Stanley Matthews play football. The three piers drew crowds for the slot machines, and the theatres along the seafront featured many big-name performers during the summer season.

The Pleasure Beach rides provided entertainment for many; others had a trip to the tower for the organ music of Reginald Dixon or ballroom dancing. For the energetic, the swimming pools proved popular while the bathing beauty competitions and shows of high-board diving were for those who just wanted to watch. Fresh air and fun was the norm but on many days, sales of pakamacs soared as the heavens opened, with soaking holidaymakers rushing into the many indoor attractions of amusement arcades, fortune tellers, bingo or the waxworks.

After the last day of the holiday the crowds who had arrived the previous week would gather on the stations awaiting trains back home, the young people sad, and their parents reflecting on how expensive the holiday had been. For the landladies of the town this was the time to have the rooms cleaned and fresh bed linen laid as other holidaymakers would soon arrive for their week of sun and fun.

All through the summer months this cycle took place until, at season's end, another attraction was on offer for tourists; switched on by a celebrity of the day these were the famous Blackpool Illuminations. Once again the excursion traffic on the railway would descend on the town, this time bringing visitors along just for the evening. Departures would be late at night with arrivals back home in the early hours.

Seaside Humour

No trip to the seaside would be complete without sending a postcard back home. The postal service was so good in those times that it would reach the addressee the next morning without fail. Some senders favoured views of coastal resorts whereas others preferred the saucy *double entendre* versions. Youngsters would try to take a peek at the sales displays before parents invoked their disapproval.

The master of postcard humour was the artist Donald McGill, his works were saucy, well drawn, and full of fun. Strongly featured were topics such as landladies, mothers-in-law, nagging wives, drunkard husbands, Scotsmen and the innocence of newly-weds. These sometimes fell foul of the local watch committee who approved the cards for sale in each resort. However, a postcard banned in one area could often be found in the next resort. Now so innocent by today's standards, the cards, many thousands of which were printed, are very collectable.

(R.S. Collection)

The Magic of the Isle of Man

Before the advent of foreign holidays, a trip to the Isle of Man was almost like going abroad. With the allure of its own unique 3ft-gauge railway system using Beyer-Peacock locomotives, horse trams and the Manx electric railway, all enthusiasts would find something of interest on the island. Another attraction for thousands of motorcyclists was, and still is, the Tourist Trophy event.

A sailing of 80 miles from Liverpool and 63 miles from Fleetwood was more than that of the short sea crossings to France or Belgium. It was from these ports that thousands of holidaymakers would board the mini-liners of the Isle of Man Steam Packet Company (IOMSPC). Services were advertised with colourful posters pasted on station walls, showcase models of the ships were also displayed on some of the North-West's station platforms.

Formed in 1830, the IOMSPC it still is the oldest shipping company in the world and pre-dates the ocean-going Cunard Company who copied the Steam Packet Company's colours of red and black for their own ships' funnels. The classic steamships in use during the 1950s and early 1960s were:

The Lady of Mann
Ben-my-Chree
King Orry
Monas Isle
Monas Queen
Snaefell
Tynwald
Manxman

Many wondered who Ben-my-Chree was, and maybe found out that it was not a person but 'Girl in my Heart' in the Manx language. All the liners have now been scrapped with the exception of the *Manxman*, built at the famous Cammell Laird shipyard at Birkenhead in 1955. The last of Britain's cross-channel steamships survives in a sorry state awaiting funding to save her from the breakers and refurbish her for the nation. Rather like the railway preservationist, a society exists to raise funds to save this piece of history from the living memory of many.

Crewe North 5A-based 'Royal Scot' no. 46148 *The Manchester Regiment* passes through Lancaster Castle station with a parcels train. The scene is pre-1958 as the tender has the early BR logo. *(Travel Lens Photographic)*

Opposite, top: Jubilee no. (4)5685 *Barfleur* gathers water from Brock Troughs with a Down Windermere train on 22 July 1937. *(H.C. Doyle/Gresley Society)*

Opposite, bottom: Racing along over Brock Troughs with scoop lowered to pick up several thousand gallons of water is the engine whose name had spotters tongue-tied, no. (4)6230 *Duchess of Buccleuch*. *(H.C. Doyle/ Gresley Society)*

The headlamp code of Crewe 5A-based 'Black 5' no. (4)5380 indicates an express goods at Bolton le Sands on 21 July 1938. Possibly Bovril sandwiches became popular with the advertising of the day. *(H.C. Doyle/ Gresley Society)*

A scene at Carnforth in the Steamtown days as preserved 'Black 5' no. (4)5407 moves between the coal and ash plants. The depot became a magnet for enthusiasts during the decline of steam and was one of the last steam sheds in use. For some years the site was a major depot for preserved locos. For those who ventured onto the station the waiting rooms would seem familiar as they were used in the film *Brief Encounter*. *(R.S. Collection)*

Opposite, bottom: Leader of the class, no. (4)6100 *Royal Scot*, carries the bell souvenir from its American Tour of 1933, through Bolton le Sands on 21 July 1938. The real identity of the loco is no. (4)6152 which was renumbered for the tour. The bell was removed when the loco was rebuilt, and no. 46100 then seemed adept at avoiding photographers in her rebuilt shape. *(H.C. Doyle/ Gresley Society)*

17

THE CLIMBS BEGIN

After Carnforth the climbs begin, firstly a short climb of 2¼ miles at 1 in 134 until Milnthorpe is reached. From Milnthorpe there is 13 miles of climbing, ranging from 1 in 106 to 1 in 175, to Grayrigg. A water pick-up at Dillicar Troughs is needed before possibly whistling by Tebay Shed 11D to pick up one one of the 2–6–4 tanks shedded there. The 1950s allocation consisted of four Fowler tank engines, four Ivatt class 4 2–6–0s and two Fowler 4F 0–6–0s. The tanks gave a push at the rear of the train on the climbs to conquer Shap Summit, which are at 1 in 145 and 4 miles at 1 in 75 to rise to 916ft above sea level. The rock cutting signals the end of the climbing and the banker will stop at the signal-box to return to 11D light-engine.

The stretch of line is a magnet mostly for adult enthusiasts as it has some of the bleakest weather conditions in the country. Windswept and rain-lashed, some camp lineside while others prefer the Junction Hotel at Tebay where the scene can be overviewed from bedroom windows. Although Scout Green signal-box is rather remote, its signalman receives many visitors. From Shap the footplate crew have a relaxing 32-mile downhill run into Carlisle Citadel station.

An excursion, seen at 5.45 p.m. on 23 July 1938, with Fowler 4F 0–6–0 no. (4)4215 in charge passes through Oxenholme. (*H.C. Doyle/Gresley Society*)

At Oxenholme on 23 July 1938, an Up double-headed express with compound 4–4–0 no. (4)1170 heading 'Royal Scot' no. (4)6115 *Scots Guardsman*. Notice how the signalman's garden is in full bloom. (*H.C. Doyle/Gresley Society*)

'Patriot' no. 45548 *Lytham St Annes* hurries an Up express along through the scenic cutting at Grayrigg at 1.00 p.m. on 13 July 1938. (*H.C. Doyle/Gresley Society*)

The Up 'Coronation Scot' hauled by no. (4)6224 *Princess Alexandra*, complete with matching coaching stock, picks up water at Dillicar Troughs. Pictured here at 4.00 p.m. on 22 July 1938, the 'Coronation Scot' only ran for two years, owing to the outbreak of war in 1939. *(H.C. Doyle/Gresley Society)*

Opposite, top: Passing through Tebay station and clearing Tebay no. 2 signal-box at 11.15 a.m. on 23 July 1938 is 'Jubilee' no. (4)5693 *Agamemnon*. The train is a Down express. *(H.C. Doyle/Gresley Society)*

Opposite, bottom: One of the ex-LMS 'Jinty' 0–6–0 tanks, no. (4)7339, heads a loose-coupled goods train through Tebay station. Although this is 1938 the scene remained the same for many years. *(H.C. Doyle/ Gresley Society)*

The discomforts of poor weather on Shap often yielded superb photographs. The BR 'Clan' class tended to stay in the north of the country and were rarities for some spotters. Here, no. 72001 *Clan Cameron* hauls an eleven-coach train over Shap. *(C. Ord/R.S. Collection)*

Opposite, top: A fitted goods train headed by 'Black 5' no. 45248 has the assistance of a banking engine on the climb up to Shap Summit on 21 April 1962. *(R.S. Collection)*

Opposite, bottom: A four-coach train should not provide too much trouble for rebuilt 'Patriot' no. 45527 *Southport* on the climb up to Shap Summit. *(C. Ord/R.S. Collection)*

18

CARLISLE CITADEL STATION

After 299 miles of travel from London Euston, our journey concludes as we enter the platforms of Carlisle Citadel station. Completed in 1850, the buildings designed by Sir William Ike are some of the masterpieces of railway architecture. The Tudor style blends in well with the city's other architecture and retains a fresh look even after 100 years of use. The circular ironwork within the station is unique and produces a strange shadow on the trains below. At the end of the train shed, large ornate roof end screens similar to those in a cathedral bear the grime from the many steam locos that have passed beneath – they were replaced before the end of the steam age.

Although the station was not bustling for most of the day it had arrivals and departures from the Settle & Carlisle line as well as local and Anglo-Scottish trains of the London Midland Region. A common sight was of two 'Pacifics' side by side; the incoming engine would uncouple from the train and make its way to Carlisle Upperby Shed 12B. Meanwhile, the wheeltapper proceeded along the coaching stock tapping each wheel and checking its bearings. A fresh engine (normally a Scottish Region 'Pacific') would back down onto the train and couple up to the stock ready for the onward journey to Glasgow Central, a further 102 miles. The hardest work for the Scottish crew would be the ascent to Beattock Summit graded between 1 in 74 and 1 in 88.

Rebuilt 'Royal Scot' no. 46162 *Queen's Westminster Rifleman* seen on 16 April 1963. At that time, no. 46162 was allocated to Carlisle Kingmoor, and had an admirer in the pipe-smoking gentleman attired in trilby and long overcoat of the times. *(R.S. Collection)*

The last LMS 'Pacific', no. 46256 *Sir William Stanier F.R.S.*, passes Crown Street goods depot with an arrival from Euston. *(Gordon Turner of Lanchester, County Durham)*

'Black 5' no. 45279, one of the 1936–8 products of Armstrong Whitworth, in rather grimy condition. The only clean part visible has been caused by an overspill of water. *(R.S. Collection)*

Carlisle Citadel not only had the west coast trains, but also those of Settle & Carlisle workings. In October 1952 'Jubilee' no. 45605 *Cyprus* heads 'Royal Scot' no. 46109 *Royal Engineer* on the Up 'Thames–Clyde Express'. *(R. Butterfield/Gresley Society)*

Opposite, top: Ex-LMS 2P 4–4–0 no. 40695 starts a local passenger train out of Citadel in June 1951 while, on the left, an ex-ER loco, possibly a B1, heads into the station. The ornate end screens bear the soot from the thousands of engines that passed underneath. *(R.S. Collection)*

Opposite, bottom: 'Jubilee' no. 45697 *Achilles* is pictured in 1965 wearing the yellow stripe that prohibits workings south of Crewe. Schoolboy spotters take in the scene from the platform seat. *(R.S. Collection)*

The sight of two locos bearing 'The Royal Scot' headboard is quite normal as Carlisle Citadel is the changeover point. The two 'Duchess' class engines are no. 46253 *City of St Albans* and no. 46223 *Princess Alice*. *(E. Haigh/R.S. Collection)*

Opposite, top: No. 46243 *City of Lancaster* has her sanders on to aid grip as she starts a lengthy train southwards. *(Gordon Turner of Lanchester, County Durham)*

Opposite, bottom: A volcanic departure shows no. 46203 *Princess Margaret Rose* with 'The Mid-Day Scot' sometime between 1956 and 1958, as the engine has acquired a separate top-feed and dome. *(Gordon Coltas)*

Although the 'Clan' class shares many similarities with the 'Britannia' class engines, their smaller boiler is noticeable on no. 72005 *Clan MacGregor*, photographed in July 1962. The engine carries the 12A shedcode of Carlisle Kingmoor where five were allocated. *(D. Loveday)*

A double-header led by 'Patriot' no. 45507 *Royal Tank Corps*, coupled to 'Royal Scot' no. 46145 which has the lengthy name of *The Duke of Wellington's Regt (West Riding)*. *(R.S. Collection)*

A sparkling clean no. 46236 *City of Bradford* of 12B Carlisle Upperby Shed gets admiring glances from the assembled spotters. *(Gordon Turner of Lanchester, County Durham)*

A common scene at Citadel with two 'Duchess' engines on view. On the left, no. 46252 *City of Leicester* waits to take over an express, while no. 46222 *Queen Mary* is ready to move off. The DMU would be of little interest to an observer. *(Gordon Turner of Lanchester, County Durham)*

Rebuilt 'Patriot' no. 45535 *Sir Herbert Walker K.C.B.* of 12A Carlisle Kingmoor waits in the centre road to take over another working in May 1963. *(D. Loveday)*

Crewe North's no. 46254 *City of Stoke-on-Trent* has express code headlamps attached in readiness to change engines and work southwards in August 1964. The yellow stripe on the cab is the ominous sign of looming electrification south of Crewe. *(D. Loveday)*

'Patriot' no. 45541 *Duke of Sutherland* of 12B Carlisle Upperby simmers ready for departure on 30 August 1958. The loco would soon be transferred to 2A Rugby Shed. *(R.S. Collection)*

The early BR logo on the tender of 'Black 5' no. 44669 dates this view to the early 1950s. *(E. Haigh/ R.S. Collection)*

The Fowler 0–6–0 Tank Engines

A class of loco to be seen at many locations on the London Midland Region was the very popular and useful 3F Fowler 0–6–0 tank engine, known by many as 'Jinty' engines (although this nickname is said to really belong to another class of tank engine). The class was introduced between 1924 and 1931 as a development from an earlier 0–6–0T design by Samuel Johnson of the Midland Railway in the 1880s. The class eventually amounted to 422 examples and were numbered between 47260 and 47681 after British Railways became nationalised in 1948. The building programme was in twenty-three batches spread around private builders with only one order originating from an LMS works. Six locos were adapted for push-pull operation; nos 47478–81 and 47655–81.

Some detail variations were also noticeable within the class. Following overhaul at Darlington, Crewe-based no. 47482 emerged with its number displayed LNER-style on its tank side beneath the BR logo, much to the dismay of many observers. Maybe Darlington did not have number transfers to fit the conventional placing?

Possibly the largest allocation of the class was forty at the former North London Railways shed of 1D Devons Road.

Spotters would find that three 'Jinty' numbers were not in their *abc* books: 47613, 47617 and 47663 – as these were casualties from the eight engines loaned to the War Department in 1940.

Builder	Year	British Railways Number
Vulcan Foundry	1924	47260 – 47279
North British	1924	47280 – 47294
Hunslet	1924	47295 – 47301
Hunslet	1925	47302 – 47309
North British	1926	47317 – 47376
Vulcan Foundry	1926	47377 – 47426
Hunslet	1926	47427 – 47435
Hunslet	1927	47436 – 47451
Bagnall	1926	47452 – 47460
Bagnall	1927	47461 – 47466
Vulcan Foundry	1928	47467 – 47471
Vulcan Foundry	1927	47472 – 47477
Vulcan Foundry	1928	47478 – 47516
Beardmore	1928	47517 – 47541
Hunslet	1927	47542 – 47549
Hunslet	1928	47550 – 47566
Hunslet	1928	47567 – 47586
Hunslet	1929	47587 – 47591
Beardmore	1928	47592 – 47601
Beardmore	1929	47602 – 47640
LMS Horwich	1931 in-house builder	47667 – 47681
Beardmore	1929	47310 – 47316 **

** Built for the Somerset & Dorset Railway as numbers 19–25

'Jinty' Survivors

British Railways Number	Builder/ Date
47279	Vulcan Foundry / 1924
47298	Hunslet / 1924
47324	North British / 1926
47327	North British / 1926
47357	North British / 1926
47383	Vulcan Foundry / 1926
47406	Vulcan Foundry / 1926
47445	Hunslet / 1927
47493	Vulcan Foundry / 1927
47564	Hunslet / 1928

One of the fortunate 3F survivors, no. 47357, now resides at the Midland Railway Centre at Butterley together with no. 47327 and long-term candidates for restoration nos 47445 and 47564.

Carlisle Upperby 12B-based 'Jinty' no. 47295 awaits its next turn of removing empty stock on 16 June 1958. The 'Jinty' class's reign at Carlisle was shortly to be brought to an end by Ivatt 4–6–2 tanks taking over their duties. *(R.S. Collection)*

Opposite, top: One of the few 'Jinty' tanks built in-house, no. 47667, an LMS Horwich-built engines, marshals the stock of a goods train in May 1963. *(D. Loveday)*

Opposite, bottom: The fireman of 'Jinty' tank no. 47408 is replenishing the tanks of his engine on 30 August 1958. Visible on the next platform is a tank from one of the many Express Dairies milk trains to be seen around Carlisle. *(R.S. Collection)*

'Jinty' no. 47292 removes empty coaching stock at the southern end of Citadel against a backdrop of the steelwork for the new end screens of the station, 30 August 1958. (*R.S. Collection*)

'Jinty' 0–6–0T no. 47326 on pilot duties at the south end of the station. In the background is the goods depot at Crown Street. (*R.S. Collection*)

An always-welcome double-header, no. 45552 *Silver Jubilee* of 5A Crewe North and an unidentified Stanier engine, May 1962. After taking water from the crane, the fireman is about to return the bag back into position. The identity of 45552 and 45642 was exchanged in April 1935 for the loco to receive chrome embellishments. The identities were never changed back. *(D. Loveday)*

Rebuilt 'Royal Scot' no. 46108 *Seaforth Highlander* has cylinder draincocks opened in readiness for a southbound departure on 12 June 1956. *(R.S. Collection)*

The tender logo reveals the date of no. 46223 *Princess Alice* heading the tartan-headboarded 'Royal Scot' as being pre-1958 when the new logo was introduced. *(E. Haigh/R.S. Collection)*

BR standard 'Britannia' class no. 70052 *Firth of Tay* is centre road in readiness to take over a northbound train on 27 July 1956. 'The Mid-Day Scot' had recently arrived, headed by no. 46243 *City of Lancaster* which still has a chamfered smoke-box. *(R.S. Collection)*

Rebuilt 'Patriot' no. 45535 *Sir Herbert Walker K.C.B.* at the head of a goods train on the outskirts of Carlisle in about 1959. The engine's home shed was 8A Liverpool Edge Hill. The open cover on the tender was not good practice as coal dust and water led to blockages with injectors. *(R.S. Collection)*

'Jubilee' no. 45678 *De Robeck* heads a long train of flat wagons in May 1962. To spotters this engine is a treat for its unique sequence of numbering. *(D. Loveday)*

'Duchess' no. 46236 *City of Bradford* heads 'The Royal Scot' past a mass of assembled goods vehicles in 1956. The massive new marshalling yards built at Carlisle in 1963 improved the handling of goods trains and could deal with 246 goods trains and 4,900 wagons in a twenty-four-hour period – a little too late an improvement with the mass exodus to road haulage. *(R.S. Collection)*

19

CARLISLE UPPERBY SHED

Coded 12B from 1948 to 1950 and 1958 to 1966.

No. 46244 *King George VI* was the loco used for the inaugural run of 'The Caledonian' on September 1957 by Camden driver Bill Starvis and fireman J. Tumalty from Carlisle to Euston. Arrival at Euston was an incredible 37 minutes ahead of schedule; this was the fastest-ever recorded southbound steam run. *(D. Loveday)*

Crewe-built in 1936, 'Jubilee' no. 45715 *Invincible*, like a few other members of the class, has the mismatched Fowler 3,500-gallon tender. It is seen here in May 1962. *(D. Loveday)*

Hughes/Fowler Crab 2–6–0 no. 42864 shows the angled running gear, which gave the class their nickname. The narrowness of the tenders fitted to the class is also evident. It is seen here in May 1962. *(D. Loveday)*

Pictured in July 1962 a Crewe-built 'Jubilee' of 1936, no. 45728 *Defiance*, coupled to a Fowler 3,500-gallon tender, shows evidence of smokebox cleaning, but still needs the ash brushing away to complete the job. 4F 0–6–0 no. 44008 alongside shows the large numbers used on Scottish-based engines. (*D. Loveday*)

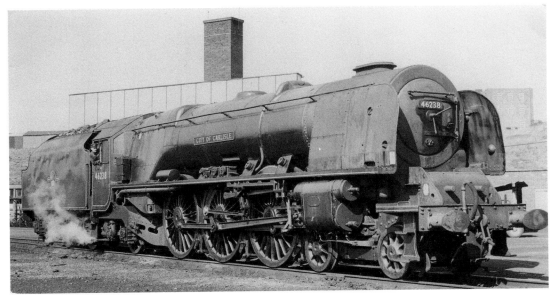

A fitting finale: no. 46238 *City of Carlisle* in readiness to come off-shed. For many years no. 46238 was a resident and pet loco of 12B Upperby. She was kept in superb condition and for a time it was rumoured she was a candidate for preservation. Unfortunately this did not occur, and she was withdrawn in September 1964 and scrapped in December of that year having achieved a recorded mileage of 1,602,628. (*R.S. Collection*)